KECHARA
A Tsem Tulku Buddhist Organisation
Media & Publications

Other titles by Tsem Tulku Rinpoche, published by Kechara Media & Publications
(in order of publication date)

108 Ways to Grab My Apples,
Tsem Tulku Rinpoche, 2010

Tsongkhapa: A Simple Guide to a Powerful Practice,
Tsem Tulku Rinpoche, 2010

Snakes, Roosters & Pigs,
Tsem Tulku Rinpoche, 2010

If Not Now, When?,
Tsem Tulku Rinpoche, 2009

Peace: A Compilation of Short Teachings,
Tsem Tulku Rinpoche, 2009

Setrap the Protector: Secrets Revealed of a 1,000-Year-Old Practice,
Tsem Tulku Rinpoche & Sharon Saw, 2009

Gurus for Hire, Enlightenment for Sale,
Tsem Tulku Rinpoche, 2009

Compassion Conquers All,
Tsem Tulku Rinpoche, 2007

Nothing Changes, Everything Changes,
Tsem Tulku Rinpoche, 2006

Faces of Enlightenment,
Tsem Tulku Rinpoche, 2006

Why I Make Myself Unhappy,
Tsem Tulku Rinpoche, 2005

Other titles published by Kechara Media & Publications

Je Tsongkhapa: A Visual Journey,
Gisbert Pascal Roth 2010

Call Me Paris,
Jamie Khoo 2009

There's No Way But Up,
David Lai, 2009

Vajrayogini and Other Sacred Power Places in Nepal,
Paul Yap & David Lai, 2009

The Illustrated Life Story of Lama Tsongkhapa: A Graphic Novel,
Terry Lim & Kok Yek Yee, 2009

Pocket Prayers: A Concise Compilation of Prayers,
Kechara, 2009

For more details or to purchase these titles, please visit **kechara.com/kmp**
Kechara Media & Publications also publish Chinese titles.

Eat Healthy, Daily

21 Traditional Chinese Vegetarian Recipes for Healing

inspired by
Tsem Tulku Rinpoche

recipes by
Dr. Jiang Zhong

Kechara Media & Publications
2011

Copyright © 2011 Kechara Media & Publications
All rights reserved. No part of this book may be used or reproduced in any manner whatsoever without written permission from Kechara Media & Publications except in the case of brief quotations embodied in critical articles and reviews.

Publisher's note: The contents in this publication is provided for general information purposes only and do not constitute, or substitute, other professional or medical advice, diagnosis, or treatment.

Kechara Media & Publications Sdn. Bhd.
41-2A & 41-2B, 1st Floor
Jalan PJU 1/3C
SunwayMas Commercial Centre
47301 Petaling Jaya
Selangor, Malaysia

Tel   : (+603) 7805 5691
Fax   : (+603) 7805 5690
Email   : kmp@kechara.com
Website : www.kechara.com/kmp

The moral right of the author has been asserted.

ISBN 978 967 5365 48 5

Andrew James Boon - Art Director
Lee Kheng San - Photographer (Kechara InMotion)
Low Kar Wai - Chinese Translator
Saras Manickam - Editor
Wong Yek Hao - Designer

Printed by
Times Offset (M) Sdn Bhd
Malaysia

CONTENT

Foreword by H.E. Tsem Tulku Rinpoche	06 - 07
Biography on the Author	08 - 09
Introduction on a little book of simple wonders	10 - 13
Recipe #1: Cabbage stir fry with chilli and ginger	14 - 15
Recipe #2: Asparagus sautéed in ginger and soy sauce	16 - 17
Recipe #3: Bean sprouts stir fry in vinegar and ginger	18 - 19
Recipe #4: Bitter gourd and tofu in black bean sauce	20 - 21
Recipe #5: Panfried eggplant with sour ginger sauce	22 - 23
Recipe #6: Broccoli florets sautéed with ginger and onion	24 - 25
Recipe #7: Cucumber mixed salad with chilli oil dressing	26 - 27
Recipe #8: Sweet potato leaves salad in spicy tangy dressing	28 - 29
Recipe #9: Sweet potato cutlets served crunchy & caramelised	30 - 31
Recipe #10: Blanched black fungus with wasabi vinaigrette	32 - 33
Recipe #11: Abalone mushroom with ginger and onion	34 - 35
Recipe #12: Spinach salad with spicy garlic dressing	36 - 37
Recipe #13: Beancurd braised with seaweed	38 - 39
Recipe #14: Bamboo shoots stir fry with broccoli florets	40 - 41
Recipe #15: Tremella fungus and lotus seed dessert	42 - 43
Recipe #16: Daylily buds – Soup of peaceful mind	44 - 45
Recipe #17: Multi bean and barley detox porridge	46 - 47
Recipe #18: Winter melon with seaweed porridge	48 - 49
The Dharma of a Vegetarian diet	50 - 51
Recipe #19: Tomato & onion scrambled omelette	52 - 53
Recipe #20: Pumpkin panfried in sweet egg batter	54 - 55
Recipe #21: Dumplings with chives and egg filling	56 - 57
Acknowledgement	58
About Kechara	59
About KMP	60
About KWPC	61
Glossary - an introduction to living healthy	62 - 64
Pull-out Glossary Poster	Special
Chinese Translations	65 - 128

FOR

H. E. Tsem Tulku Rinpoche
Spiritual Guide of Kechara Buddhist Organisation

WORD
by H.E. Tsem Tulku Rinpoche

In modern life, food is synthetically created and made so convenient that we can literally buy everything ready-packed and processed; all we need to do is heat it up and eat it. We end up sacrificing the health aspect in what we eat. I am also guilty of this and I have suffered some health issues as a result of my diet. I am sure there are many others out there who have experienced the same.

I have come across a wonderful doctor who is good in cooking, excellent in acupuncture and wonderful in treating many of my medical problems. By following his advice and treatments, I have experienced some good results. One day, as I was talking with this doctor we chanced upon the subject of whether he can cook, and he said that he could. He explained that there was not a lot of meat in the village he grew up in so the people there were vegetarian. They learnt to cook the vegetables they had in various combinations, which turned out to be quite delicious.

In traditional Chinese medicine, which has grown tremendously in popularity all over the world, the balance of the Yin (coolness) and the Yang (heat) is very important for our body to be healthy. The recipes featured in this book are designed specifically to balance the Yin and the Yang in our individual bodies. I personally found the dishes to be very delicious, very light and, although they were filling, did not leave me with a bloated feeling whatsoever.

I felt I would like to bring these wonderful, ancient, healing and special recipes to the world at large. I thought that this book would benefit a lot of people who are particular about their taste buds, and who would like meals which are healthy, very easy to make and economical, because none of these dishes are expensive at all.

I would like everybody to have good health, to be free of pain and medical problems and to have a very long life. I hope everyone will enjoy these wonderful recipes from a great traditional Chinese doctor, my friend Dr. Jiang. Thank you very much.

Tsem Rinpoche

BIOGRAPHY
on the Author

Born in China in 1975, Dr Jiang Zhong is a graduate of Chang Chun College in Jilin Province. He developed a passion for traditional Chinese medicine from childhood, studying a wide range of theories from various traditional and professional sources. As a practitioner with extensive practical experience, he was appointed panel practitioner for twelve Chinese medicine stores in Taonan city of Jilin Province. His work involved making up prescriptions and advising on traditional Chinese medicine treatment. Dr Jiang had his own clinics for two years, where he had to deal with a wide spectrum of challenging cases. His exposure to, investigation into and treatment of the various health issues during his clinical practice, honed his skills as a traditional Chinese medicine practitioner.

In 2001, Dr Jiang founded a natural therapy health centre to provide natural therapies to enhance health and prevent illness without the use of drugs. The centre provided therapies such as qigong, acupuncture, tui-na (Chinese bodywork massage), gua-sha (skin scraping), moxibustion (treatment to dispel cold and dampness from the body) and external application of medicine. In combination with dietary therapy, Dr Jiang's natural therapies have proven effective for a large number of complex and difficult problems. In the same year, Dr Jiang also founded a tui-na school in Taonan City, Jilin Province. The school has trained and produced many excellent tui-na students to serve the community.

Since 2005, Dr Jiang has been a regular visitor to Southeast Asian countries, particularly Singapore, Malaysia, Thailand and Vietnam in his capacity as a traditional Chinese medicine consultant. He is a specialist in brain and blood vessel related treatments (the after effect of strokes), diabetes and neck and shoulders syndrome. He also focuses on therapies that invigorate the physical and psychological health of cancer patients.

Dr Jiang always promotes diagnosis as per Western medicine followed by treatment using Chinese medicine which has no chemical side effects. He strongly believes that any kind of pent up stress or pressure in the body such as blood clots, phlegm, body heat or trapped gas is bad for health. One major culprit for city folks is constipation. It is essential to clear these 'obstructions' to make way for healthy new energy. This is the core reason why this book emphasizes the need for detoxification.

09

INTRODUCTION
on a little book of simple wonders

This is a recipe book of simple vegetarian dishes. It is also more than that. It is a book of strategies to successfully combat modern civilisation's health ills, including cancer, diabetes and obesity. One drawback of modern development and progress has been the increased onset of 'rich men's' health issues such as diabetes and obesity. Poor eating habits and too much processed food are hardly conducive to good health. Obesity, as well as diabetes, with attendant problems is on the rise. Cancer, no respecter of status, hits at everyone, rich and poor.

Western medication with drugs and perhaps invasive treatment is of course the most common solution for these diseases. Traditional Chinese medicine however, advocates a multi-pronged approach that involves healing the body from within. This includes first detoxing the body of its accrued toxicity; then nourishing and replenishing the internal organs, equipping them with strength to fight disease.

Healthy foods such as fruits and vegetables are natural medicines that have their own distinct medicinal properties and functions. Learning how to use natural dietary practices to prevent common health problems becomes a powerful tool to enhance good health.

Rinpoche says, "People sometimes forget to take their medication but they never forget to eat. It's human nature. We must have our meals every single day. If the food we consume can help cure illness, then this food is better than any kind of medicine."

Consuming vegetables as medicine? It sounds far-fetched and many people are naturally sceptical. However, there are too many proven success stories to dismiss this theory out of hand. The effect of food dietary treatments has been absolutely phenomenal compared to prescriptive medicine. For example, black fungus and white fungus help to naturally unclog blood vessels and arteries. In the Western medical world, the solution would perhaps be a surgical procedure such as angioplasty to treat clogged arteries in the heart. Apart from unclogging arteries, black fungus also helps to reduce the cholesterol level and ease constipation. Asparagus is commonly known as the best food to fight cancer.

In China, asparagus extract is used in medical treatment for cancer. Cabbage is used to cure gastric ulcers and is good for wound healing. Chinese spinach is known for nourishing the blood and easing constipation. Celery assists in lowering the blood pressure.

The list goes on. Sweet potatoes, both tubers and leaves are an amazing storehouse of varied nutrients to combat many diseases. Cucumbers, winter melons, eggplants and more – all the vegetables featured in this book are warriors. Each is armed with a cache of vitamins, minerals and phytochemicals to replenish, nourish and strengthen our internal organs as well as to fight health problems.

All this is well and good. However, be on your guard against monotony and fried foods.

A monotonous diet is 'challenging' in the long run.
It is boring to eat the same food every day. Sometimes, people consume a certain vegetable to treat a specific illness. Inevitably, after a while, they get sick and tired of eating it day after day. They give up and resort to Western medicine instead. That is why patients are encouraged to have a variety of palatable foods (that have medicinal properties) rather than stick to a monotonous diet.

Fried foods release fire toxins which are harmful to health.
We all know that fried food is bad for health. The main reason is because cooking at high temperatures produces cancer-causing chemicals. People in the olden days didn't understand this but they somehow managed to figure out the fire toxin theory.

During the years of concocting and preparing various types of medicine I discovered that patients often suffered from internal heat after consuming medicine which had been cooked for a longer period of time. This problem of internal heat, however, can be resolved by using special preparatory methods.

Three ancient methods for releasing fire toxins are:
1) Seal up the concoction in a ceramic pot and place it in a well for two to three days.
2) Leave the concoction on the ground of a dry and cool area or bury it underground.
3) Cream type medicine for external use can be soaked in cold water.

Using the above methods for foods that need longer cooking time will help resolve the problem of internal heat. Ordinarily, health foods should not cause internal heat, but many practitioners perhaps do not follow the above methods while developing herbal extracts, and consequently, the toxic fire trapped in food does not get eliminated.

Remove toxic heat trapped in food, in the comfort of your own home.
In the case of liquid medicine, remove the cap and keep in the chiller section of your refrigerator for 3 to 4 days. Medicine for external application will cause red rashes if the fire toxins have not been released. Use the methods mentioned above to release them. When you follow these procedures, there is no harm in enjoying fried and baked food occasionally. They may even help to warm your body.

Go vegetarian.
A well-planned vegetarian diet that includes vegetables, fungus, sea vegetables and beans is a healthy approach to meet your nutritional needs.

Regular healthy eating habits.
Healthy eating habits are developed when you consume proper food taken in the right quantity at the right time, which means you should eat on time, not when you feel hungry. Bad habits such as skipping breakfast and eating before sleeping will negatively affect our health. Portion control is also essential. Stop eating when you are 80% full.

Medical effects of seasonings.

Many people are unaware that most seasonings are heaty, especially the seasonings for steamboat soup and marinated meat. You find them everywhere in China. Some people develop diabetes after consuming such dishes every day for couple of years. The toxic heat in such seasonings affects the normal functions of internal organs. Many people think that this is a common problem due to over consumption of meat. The main culprit is actually the seasonings.

To illustrate, star anise, cumin, tsaoko amomum (black cardamom, cao guo), cinnamon, cloves, nutmeg, pepper, Sichuan pepper, ginger, onions, garlic and chilli are all heaty spices. The combination of these spices makes for a very tasty seasoning for meat. Moderate consumption of these seasonings will help clear the dampness in the body. For those who love cold drinks, these seasonings will help to protect the stomach.

The benefits of seasonings such as vinegar, soy sauce, onions, garlic and ginger can be found in our pull-out Glossary Poster.

The recipes in this book.

All recipes were selected based on certain criteria. For instance, the vegetables used are among the most superior disease fighters with distinct medicinal properties. The range of vegetables keeps monotony to a minimum. All the dishes require very little preparation time. The ingredients are easily available. Cooking is relatively simple. Importantly, emphasis is on detoxification, followed by nourishing, replenishing and healing. As mentioned earlier, vegetables are natural medicines. This book offers a cooking perspective on them.

We hope you will have as much pleasure trying out the recipes as we had in putting this book together.

Eat well and good health!

CABBAGE

STIR FRY
with chilli and ginger

Brassica oleracea (bao cai)

The cabbage is an ancient vegetable that originated about 4000 years ago. It was known to the Greeks and Romans as well as Chinese and Indians. Early Chinese jade carvings with cabbage motifs indicate that the cabbage represented wealth and prosperity. In both Europe and Asia, it has a long history associated with food, medicine and medical folklore. For instance, breast feeding mothers wrap cabbage leaves over their breasts to relieve the pain of engorgement.

Ingredients:

500g cabbage roughly chopped
2 inch ginger thinly sliced
2 cloves garlic finely chopped
6 pieces dried chilli cut in half
1 tsp Sichuan pepper
4 tbsp vegetable oil

½ tbsp soy sauce
1 tbsp brown rice vinegar
½ tbsp brown sugar
1 ½ tsp corn flour
200ml water
salt to taste

Method:

1) Mix soy sauce, vinegar, sugar, corn flour, water and salt to form a seasoning sauce.
2) Heat oil in pan. Sauté the ginger, garlic, chilli and Sichuan pepper until fragrant.
3) Add the cabbage. Stir-fry briskly. When the cabbage begins to wilt, pour in the seasoning sauce. Stir-fry for a few seconds. Dish up and serve immediately.
4) This recipe emphasises very quick, high heat cooking. Overcooking destroys the healing properties of cabbage. As such, time the cooking just right and avoid overcooking.

Benefits:

In traditional Chinese medicine, the cabbage is used to heal wounds and gastrointestinal ulcers, relieve constipation, cleanse and detoxify as well as to induce weight loss. It is an important ingredient for treating atherosclerosis, gallstones and ulcers.

Side Effects:

Those who have a weak spleen and stomach may experience symptoms of diarrhea. To avoid this, follow the ingredients in this recipe to balance the properties of cabbage.

ASPARAGUS

SAUTÉED
in ginger and soy sauce

Asparagus officinalis (lu sun)

Asparagus has an ancient history, having been recorded in the earliest recipe book ever found, written by Apicius in the 3rd century. There is even asparagus on an Egyptian frieze dated 3000 B.C. Louis XVI of France had it specially grown in hot houses in his palace grounds. White asparagus comes from the same plant as the usual green; it is grown under cover to keep the stems white. China, while being the largest producer, is the second largest exporter in the world, next to Peru.

Ingredients:

300g asparagus
1 tbsp soy sauce
3 tbsp vegetable oil

1 inch ginger thinly sliced
salt to taste with a pinch of brown sugar

Method:

1) Clean and rinse the asparagus. Cut into pieces of approx. 1.5 inches in length.
2) Boil a pot of water. Blanch the asparagus in the boiling water for 1 minute. Remove and drain. It is important not to overcook it for it turns mushy.
3) Heat the oil in a wok. Sauté the ginger till fragrant. Add the soy sauce followed by the asparagus. Stir-fry briskly.
4) Before dishing up, add salt to taste and a pinch of sugar. Serve immediately.

Benefits:

Asparagus is very cooling. Traditional Chinese medicine uses it to reduce body heat and as a diuretic. Consumed regularly, it helps alleviate heart disease, hypertension, tachycardia (a heart disorder where the heart rate is too fast), fatigue, edema (swelling caused by fluid retention) cystitis (inflammation of the bladder) and dysuria (painful urination). It is also claimed that asparagus is highly effective in the treatment of cardiovascular disease, vascular sclerosis, nephritis, gallstones, liver dysfunction and obesity. This delicate vegetable contains more vitamins and trace elements than many other vegetables. Nutritionists and vegetarians tout asparagus as not only a healthy food but also a natural food that helps prevent cancer. Many traditional healers use asparagus as a medicine for lymphoma, bladder tumours, lung tumours, kidney stones, skin cancer and leukaemia.

Side Effects:

There are no side effects in consuming asparagus.

BEAN SPROUTS

STIR FRY
in vinegar and ginger

Phaseolus aureus (dou ya)

Which vegetable is a storehouse of nutrients, needs neither soil nor fertiliser, grows anywhere in the world and requires just 3 to 5 days of growth before it is ready to be eaten? The humble bean sprout, of course! The ancient Chinese knew all about it for the Emperor Shen Nung wrote about it in 1282 B.C. Shen Nung is regarded as the Father of Chinese agriculture as well as Father of Chinese medicine.

Ingredients:

300g bean sprouts (washed and drained)
1 inch ginger thinly sliced
½ medium onion thinly sliced
½ tsp sea salt
½ tsp brown sugar

1 tbsp vegetable oil
1 tbsp soy sauce
4 tbsp vinegar

Method:

1) Heat up pan with oil. Sauté the ginger and onion until fragrant. When lightly browned add in soy sauce.
2) Turn up the heat and add in bean sprouts followed by salt and sugar (diluted in a little water). Stir for about 30 seconds.
3) Lastly add in vinegar and continue to stir well for a few more seconds. At this point you will notice a pungent sour smell. Remove from heat, dish up and serve immediately.

Benefits:

Bean sprouts are constitutionally slightly cooling. They aid detoxification and act as a diuretic as well as a laxative. Traditional healers use them to treat conjunctivitis (red eyes), sore throat and mouth ulcers. It is claimed bean sprouts help lower blood pressure, soften blood vessels, relieve constipation and prevent cancer.

Side Effects:

Bean sprouts are not easy to digest, being a cooling food. It is best that those with a weak spleen and stomach avoid it.

BITTER

GOURD AND TOFU
in black bean sauce

Momordica charantia (ku gua)

Known as King of Bitter Foods, the bitter gourd has a special place in traditional medicine from China and India to the Amazon and Sahara. The famous Chinese physician and pharmacologist, Li Shizhen (1518-1593 A.D.) in his Bencao Gangmu, or Compendium of Materia Medica, described this vegetable as "bitter in taste, non-toxic, expelling evil heat, relieving fatigue and illuminating".

Ingredients:

2pcs bitter gourd (cut into inch long strips)
3pcs soft tofu cut into small cubes
3 tbsp black bean paste
1 inch ginger thinly sliced
2 tbsp soy sauce
salt to taste with a pinch of brown sugar
½ medium onion thinly sliced
2 tbsp vegetable oil
1 tbsp brown sugar
200ml filtered water

Method:
1) Heat up oil in pan. Sauté the onion and ginger till lightly browned.
2) Add soy sauce, black bean paste, sugar and stir fry till fragrant.
3) Add the bitter gourd. Stir fry briskly. Add a little water and salt. Add the tofu, turn down the heat and let it stew for 10 minutes.
4) Lastly, add in a pinch salt and sugar. Dish up and serve immediately.

Benefits:
The bitter gourd has cooling yin energy. It helps to reduce body heat, detoxify the system and improve eyesight. Traditional healers use it to treat boils and swelling. It is claimed that the bitter gourd can help prevent cancer. It is one of the best food options for those on a diet as it is recognized worldwide as a fat killer.

Side Effects:
With its cooling energy, bitter gourd might weaken our spleen and stomach. It must be avoided during pregnancy.

PANFRIED

EGGPLANT
with sour ginger sauce

Solanum melongena (qie zi)

Indigenous to a wide belt encompassing India, China, Burma, Southeast Asia, Laos and Vietnam, the eggplant is known by many names: aubergine, derived from French and of course brinjal which is Portuguese in origin. It has been cultivated in Asia from antiquity. Arab merchants carried it to Europe while the Spanish and Portuguese introduced it to South America.

Ingredients:

4 medium sized eggplants
1 red onion finely chopped
3 inch ginger finely chopped
salt to taste with a pinch of brown sugar

3 tbsp vegetable oil
4 tsp black bean paste
3 cloves garlic finely chopped
100ml filtered water

Method:

1) Wash and dry eggplants well. Use whole with skin. Discard the stalks.
2) Heat up oil in pan. Pan fry at low heat until skin turns golden brown and crispy. Keep turning eggplants till evenly browned and soft on the inside.
3) Add the ginger, onion, garlic and black bean paste and stir fry till fragrant. Be careful not to break the skin of the eggplant.
4) Add water and let simmer at low heat for another 10 minutes. Add salt to taste and a pinch of brown sugar. Garnish with finely chopped garlic, onion and cucumber before serving.

Benefits:

The eggplant is regarded as cooling. It helps reduce body heat and is used to stop bleeding, swelling and pain. Generally, traditional healers use it to heal various types of ulcers, relieve constipation, and treat hypertension (high blood-pressure). The eggplant skin is loaded with nutrients. Among cancer fighting vegetables, the eggplant is ranked seventh.

Side Effects:

Brinjals can weaken the spleen and stomach due to its cooling properties. It is preferable that those with asthma avoid consuming it.

BROCCOL

FLORETS SAUTÉED
with ginger and onion

Brassica oleracea (xi lan hua)

Broccoli is one of those super vegetables that come ready packaged with an army of disease-fighting warriors such as anti-oxidants and phyto-chemicals. It probably originated in Italy some 2000 years ago as a species of wild cabbage.

Ingredients:
300g broccoli cut into individual florets
1 medium red onion cut in half and thinly sliced
2 inch ginger thinly sliced
1 tbsp soy sauce
2 tbsp vegetable oil
salt to taste with a pinch of brown sugar

Method:
1) Wash broccoli well and blanch in boiling water for 1 minute. The colour of the broccoli will change to a brighter green. Remove and place immediately in a bowl of cold water. Drain and set aside.
2) Heat oil in pan and sauté the ginger and onion till fragrant before adding soy sauce.
3) Add the broccoli. Stir-fry briskly to mix all the ingredients thoroughly. Add salt to taste with a pinch of brown sugar. Serve immediately.

Benefits:
Broccoli is a cooling vegetable. Traditional Chinese medicine indicates that it is consumed to strengthen kidneys, bones, spleen, brain and stomach. It is tonic food to invigorate a frail physique and reduce humming in the ears (tinnitus). Broccoli is also prescribed for memory lapses as well as to cleanse the blood vessels of impurities. As warrior-vegetable, this cruciferous ranks third among all the vegetables that prevent and fight cancer.

Side effects:
Prolonged cooking at high temperatures destroys much of the nutritional value in broccoli. Eating it raw or lightly cooked is best.

CUCUMBER

MIXED SALAD
with chilli oil dressing

Cucumis sativus (huang gua)

The cucumber originated in India and has been cultivated for over 3000 years in western Asia. When it was first introduced to China in the 2nd century B.C., it was called hu gua but in later years, during the rule of Shi Le, it was forbidden to use the word 'hu' (which means foreign) and so hu gua became huang gua. The use of cucumber as a medicinal product in China was first recorded in the 7th century.

Ingredients:

300g cucumber finely sliced
200g dried bean curd sliced
60g enoki mushrooms
50g fensi (glass noodles)
5 cloves garlic finely chopped
2 tbsp brown rice vinegar
4 tbsp vegetable oil
1 tbsp Sichuan pepper
2 tbsp chilli flakes
20g Chinese parsley roughly chopped
salt to taste with a pinch of brown sugar

Method:
1) Cut off roots of enoki mushrooms and blanch in boiling water for 30 seconds. Drain and set aside.
2) Soak fensi till soft (5 minutes) in boiling water. Drain and set aside.
3) To make the chilli oil, heat oil in wok. Sauté the sliced Sichuan pepper in the oil until the pepper turns golden brown. Remove and discard the pepper.
4) In a large salad bowl, toss items from 1) and 2) with remaining ingredients. Add salt to taste and a pinch of brown sugar. Pour chilli oil over before serving.

Benefits:
In traditional Chinese medicine, the cucumber is regarded as cooling. It is used to dissipate body heat, quench thirst, treat sore throat and fever. As well, it is used to lose weight. It is believed that the nutrients in the cucumber help inhibit the growth of tumours. Among all the anti-cancer vegetables, cucumber is ranked thirteenth.

Side effects:
Those with a weak spleen and stomach might experience diarrhoea if they consume cucumber.

SWEET POTATO

LEAVES SALAD
in spicy tangy dressing

Ipomoea batatas (fan shu ye)

Sweet potato leaves carry the same benefits as sweet potato tubers (see page 31), minus side effects such as abdominal distension and increase in stomach acid.

Ingredients:

200g sweet potato leaves
1 tbsp brown rice vinegar
1 tbsp vegetable oil
salt to taste with a pinch of black pepper
1 tbsp soy sauce
1 tsp wasabi
½ tbsp Sichuan pepper

Method:
1) First heat oil in pan, add Sichuan pepper and stir fry for a few seconds. Remove from heat and pour flavoured oil into bowl (use sieve). Set aside.
2) Blanch sweet potato leaves in boiling water for 30 seconds. Remove and dunk into bowl of water at room temperature. Drain. Add salt to taste.
3) Place the sweet potato leaves in a salad bowl. Mix the chilli oil, soy sauce, vinegar and wasabi together. Toss with sweet potato leaves and serve.

Benefits:
Herbal medicine practitioners consider that in some cases, sweet potato leaves are more effective than the tubers themselves. Indeed, the leaves are rich in antioxidants with the added bonus of chlorophyll which is being increasingly researched for cancer therapy. Traditional medicine practitioners claim that the different compounds in the leaves help to prevent cancer, reduce weight and aid detoxification. Sweet potato leaves are also beneficial for people who suffer from diabetes.

Side effects:
A major problem is that cooking destroys much of the nutrients in sweet potato leaves. Blending the raw leaves into juice effectively keeps the nutrients intact; however, the juice is not exactly delicious! A better alternative would be to blend the juice with fruit juice to mask the raw taste.

SWEET POTATO

CUTLETS SERVED
crunchy & caramelised

Ipomoea batatas (fan shu)

The humble sweet potato is beginning to reveal itself as an amazing storehouse of health benefits. Long considered the poor man's alternative to rice, it is among the most nutritious sources of complex carbohydrates, fibre, beta carotene, vitamins and minerals. It has outstanding antioxidant and anti-inflammatory benefits and though sweet in taste, actually helps regulate blood sugar.

Ingredients:

500g sweet potatoes
5 tbsp vegetable oil
2 tbsp sesame seeds

50g brown sugar
½ cup hot water

Method:

1) Wash and scrub clean the sweet potatoes and cut into cubes. Fry until golden brown. Remove the oil, leaving just one tablespoonful.
2) Melt the sugar in the hot water. Pour it in the pan with the fried potato cubes. Add sesame seeds. Keep stirring to thoroughly coat the cubes with the sugar syrup and sesame seeds. Dish out and serve immediately. Do not overcook the sugar as it will make the dish bitter.
3) Wipe the surface of the serving dish with a dollop of oil to prevent the cubes from sticking to the plate. **TIP:** As the sweet potato cubes may stick to your teeth, lightly dip the cubes into iced water before eating.

Benefits:

Sweet potatoes are yin tubers, consumed to reduce heatiness and cool down the body. Some sources claim it is the world's number one food to prevent cancer. Sweet potatoes are recommended for constipation. It is among the best foods to consume for detoxification and weight loss.

Side effects:

Sweet potatoes can cause abdominal distension and increase stomach acid. However, these problems are considerably alleviated if the tubers are well cooked. Another alternative is to serve with a glass of water or fruit juice.

BLANCHED

BLACK FUNGUS
with wasabi vinaigrette

Auricularia auricula (hei mu er)

Known by many names including cloud ear and wood ear, black fungus has been used in Chinese cuisine for centuries. With very little flavour of its own, black fungus tends to absorb the flavours of the other ingredients it is cooked with, while maintaining its crunchy texture.

Ingredients:
80g dried black fungus
1 ½ tsp soya sauce
5 tbsp brown rice vinegar
1 tbsp wasabi

Method:
1) Soak the dried fungus in hot water until soft (approximately 20 minutes). Rinse and drain.
2) Combine the soya sauce, vinegar and wasabi to make a dipping sauce.
3) Arrange black fungus and dipping sauce on a platter. This dish is great as an appetiser.

Benefits:
Rich in minerals, vitamins and amino-acids, black fungus is considered a neutral food (with balanced yin and yang). It significantly inhibits blood clotting, improves viscosity of the blood and reduces high blood pressure. The collagen in black fungus helps cleanse the digestive system, ridding the body of impurities while the polysaccharides present, play an important role in cancer prevention.

Side Effects:
There are no side effects in consuming black fungus.

ABALONE

MUSHROOM
with ginger and onion

Pleurotus abalonus (bao yu gu)

For centuries, mushrooms have been eaten for medicinal purposes, especially in China, Japan, Korea and East European and Baltic countries. The abalone mushroom, a variation of the oyster mushroom, has a velvety texture. As for shape and flavour, the mushroom resembles – yes, abalones.

Ingredients:
300g abalone mushrooms
1 red onion cut in half and thinly sliced
2 inch piece ginger thinly sliced
1 tbsp soy sauce
3 tbsp vegetable oil
salt to taste with a pinch of brown sugar

Method:
1) Boil water in a pan. Add the abalone mushrooms. Blanch for 2 minutes. Blanching enhances the taste of the mushrooms. Remove and drain.
2) Heat oil in pan and sauté the ginger and onion till fragrant.
3) Add the soy sauce and the abalone mushrooms. Stir-fry briskly. Add salt to taste. Before dishing up, add a pinch of sugar. Serve immediately.

Benefits:
Traditional Chinese medicine holds that the abalone mushroom helps to significantly reduce high blood pressure and cholesterol. It is nourishment for general well-being.

Side Effects:
The abalone mushroom contains a small amount of purine which can be broken down to form uric acid. As such, it may not be recommended for those suffering from gout. In such cases, it is advised to eat more fruits and green leafy vegetables while occasionally consuming abalone mushrooms in moderation.

SPINACH

SALAD
with spicy garlic dressing

Spinacia oleracea (bo cai)

The original home of spinach was Persia (Iran), where it was called aspanakh. Spinach found its way to China in 647 A.D. when the King of Nepal gave the Chinese Emperor a gift of the vegetable. The Moors took it to Europe in the 11th century while much later, over in America, Popeye the sailorman helped popularize spinach among 20th century children.

Ingredients:

200g spinach
4 cloves garlic finely chopped
1 tbsp chilli flakes
1 tbsp Sichuan pepper

2 tbsp vegetable oil
1 tbsp brown rice vinegar
salt to taste with a pinch of brown sugar

Method:

1) Wash and rinse the spinach. Blanch the spinach in boiling water for 30 seconds. Remove and cool in a bowl full of water at room temperature. Drain and set aside.
2) Chop the spinach into bite sized pieces. Place in a salad bowl.
3) Season with vinegar, salt and sugar.
4) To make the chilli oil, heat oil in wok. Sauté the sliced Sichuan pepper in the oil until the pepper turns golden brown. Remove and discard the pepper. Add chilli flakes and garlic into the still hot oil and mix well.
5) Drizzle the chilli oil mix on the spinach. Toss and serve immediately.

Benefits:

Spinach is of benefit in cases of hypertension, constipation, anaemia and skin allergies. Diabetics are highly recommended to consume spinach as it helps reduce the sugar level in blood.

Side Effects:

It is advisable for those with kidney problems to refrain from frequent consumption of spinach. Spinach is rich in oxalic acid which affects the absorption of calcium. To reduce the oxalic acid without destroying the nutrients, blanch the spinach in boiling water instead of cooking it.

BEANCURD

BRAISED
with seaweed

Bean curd (dou fu)

Beancurd is of ancient origin. It is said that it was invented in about 164 B.C. by Lord Liu An of the Han Dynasty. It was already well established as a food product by the time Li Shizhen (1518-1593 A.D.) published his Bencao Gangmu, a comprehensive traditional Chinese medicine book that listed all plants, animals, minerals and other items said to have medicinal value.

Ingredients:

250g beancurd (semi hard) cut into cubes
20g dried seaweed (kelp)
1 red onion cut in half and sliced
2 inch ginger thinly sliced

3 tbsp vegetable oil
3 star anise
1.5 litre filtered water
salt to taste

Method:

1) Soak the dried seaweed in water for 3 hours. Wash, rinse and cut.
2) Blanch beancurd in boiling water for about 1 minute to remove any impurities. Drain and set aside.
3) Heat the oil in a pan. Sauté the ginger and onion till fragrant. Add the seaweed and beancurd. Stir-fry briskly.
4) Add water and the star anise to the mixture. Once the mixture boils, turn down the flame. Stew for 30 minutes. Add salt to taste and serve immediately.

Benefits:

Beancurd is cholesterol-free. It helps to reduce body heat, warm the stomach and aid detoxification. Beancurd is highly recommended for reducing high blood pressure (hypertension). It is said to alleviate heart disease and arteriosclerosis as well as prevent cancer. It is among the best natural foods, containing both calcium and protein.

Side Effects:

Beancurd is not easy to digest. Those with a weak spleen and stomach should avoid it. Beancurd also contains purine. Gout sufferers should consume it in moderation with plenty of green vegetables.

BAMBOO SHOOTS

STIR FRY
with broccoli florets

Bambusa (zhu sun)

China has a relationship with the bamboo that stretches back to antiquity. From food, bedding and implements to construction materials, medicine and poetic muse, the bamboo has always been part of the psyche of the people. The crisp and tender bamboo shoots have figured prominently in Chinese cuisine and medicine for thousands of years.

Ingredients:

200g bamboo shoots
150g broccoli
1 red onion halved and quartered
2 inch ginger thinly sliced

3 tbsp vegetable oil
2 tbsp soy sauce
salt to taste with a pinch of brown sugar

Method:

1) Immerse the bamboo shoots in boiling water for 2 minutes. Drain, rinse and slice thin. If using canned bamboo shoots, wash, drain and set aside. Cut the broccoli into florets. Blanch in boiling water. Drain and keep aside.
2) Heat the oil in a pan. Sauté the ginger and onion till fragrant.
3) Add the slices of bamboo shoots and broccoli florets. Stir-fry briskly.
4) Add soy sauce and salt. Stir-fry for few more seconds. Add a pinch of sugar and serve immediately.

Benefits:

Bamboo shoots are slightly cooling in nature. They are effective in reducing body heat and removing phlegm. They help improve the digestive system. Take bamboo shoots to lose weight! Traditionally, bamboo shoots are used to promote and improve intestinal peristalsis action and prevent constipation. They also help prevent colorectal cancer.

Side Effects:

There are no side effects in consuming bamboo shoots.

TREMELLA

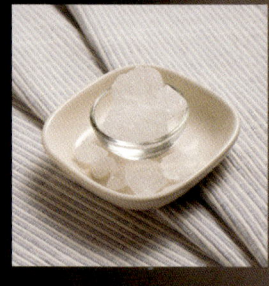

FUNGUS
and lotus seed dessert

White fungus - Tremella fuciformis (bai mu er)

Discovered growing wild in Sichuan some 200 years ago, white fungus or snow fungus as it is sometimes called, is now cultivated in mountainous regions in China. It is an important component in many Chinese herbal remedies and often taken as a beauty supplement to make the skin soft and supple. Sweeter than black fungus although its texture is similar, white fungus is sometimes called 'the poor man's bird's nest'.

Ingredients:
80g tremella fungus
300ml filtered water
2 cubes rock sugar (depending on your sweet tooth)
10 lotus seeds

Method:
1) Peel and discard the pithy stalks of the fungus. Soak the fungus in hot water until it turns white. Wash, rinse and drain.
2) Soak lotus seeds to soften them. As the pit of the seeds is bitter, it may be removed. However it is perfectly safe to eat and helps to reduce body heat.
3) Place all the ingredients into a small cooking pot and bring to a boil.
4) Turn down the heat. Simmer for 15-20 minutes and it is ready to serve.

Benefits:
Generally regarded as a tonic to nourish internal organs, nutritious white fungus enhances the efficiency of antibodies in our immune system while inhibiting tumour formation. Laboratory examinations have also shown that it prevents the depletion of white blood cells in chemotherapy patients. White fungus is used in traditional Chinese medicine to treat cough and heart palpitations. Chinese medicine maintains that white fungus treats yin deficiency by replenishing body fluid and nourishing the blood. When one suffers from lethargy and lacks sleep, yin energy food is consumed to counteract yang heatiness and to strengthen the immune system.

Side Effects:
There are no known side effects found in Tremella fungus.

DAYLILY

BUDS
soup of peaceful mind

Hemerocallis fulva (jin zhen)

Flower buds have been used in Chinese cuisine for centuries. The Chinese harvest daylily buds for cooking as well as for medicine, calling them gum jum or golden needles. The flowers last just one day, hence the name. The buds are harvested when they are 3 to 5 inches long and dried. Once dry, they turn gold in colour. The strands are knotted in the middle before cooking to bring out the flavour.

Ingredients:

- 1 cup daylily buds
- 1 cup bamboo shoots sliced
- 3 dried shiitake mushroom sliced
- 50g tremella fungus
- 20g spina date seeds
- 50g fensi (glass noodles)
- salt to taste with a pinch of brown sugar
- 1 inch ginger thinly sliced
- 3 tsp brown rice vinegar
- 1 tsp salt
- 3 tsp cornflour
- 1 tsp black pepper
- 1 litre of vegetable stock

Method:

1) Bring to boil 1 cup of water in a pot. Add the spina date seeds and simmer for 20 mins. Remove seeds and set the infused liquid aside.
2) Soak dried shiitake mushrooms, fensi and daylily buds separately in hot water till soft. Drain and set aside. Peel and discard the pithy stalks of the fungus. Soak in hot water until it turns white. Wash, rinse and drain.
3) In a large pot, mix all ingredients except the cornflour and cook for 30 mins. Mix cornflour with a little water to form a starchy paste and add into the soup towards the end. Stir well, dish out and serve.

Benefits:

Daylily buds are neutral in constitution. It is believed that they nourish the liver, act as a diuretic, help reduce swelling and soothe the nerves. Traditional healers use them to treat dizziness, tinnitus, insomnia and palpitations. In Chinese medicine, daylily buds are believed to improve brain functions as well.

Side Effects:

Daylily buds contain colchicine, a toxic and therefore harmful substance. It is however, easily eliminated when the buds are cooked thoroughly.

MULTI BEAN

# AND BARLEY
detox porridge

The Emperor Shen Nung, a mythical figure in Chinese history, decreed in 2853 B.C. that 5 plants were sacred: rice, wheat, millet, barley and soya. Barley (Hordeum vulgare) is an excellent source of dietary fibre. Cooling in nature, it aids detoxification apart from strengthening the spleen. Soy beans (Glycine max), native to China, has been cultivated for over 5000 years. Cooling and a superb source of protein, it detoxifies and lubricates the lungs and intestines. Black beans, green beans and red beans belong to the Phaselous vulgaris family. They pack a nutritional punch of fibre, protein, antioxidants, minerals and vitamins.

Ingredients:
20g black beans
20g soy beans
40g mung beans
40g red beans
40g barley
200g sweet potato
1 litre water
salt to taste

Method:
1) Wash rinse and soak (with enough water to cover) the beans and barley together for about 30 mins prior to cooking. Drain and set aside.
2) Peel, wash and cut sweet potatoes into bite sized cubes.
3) Place all the ingredients in a pot. Cover with water. Once the water boils, reduce the heat. Let the porridge simmer in low heat until all the ingredients are thoroughly cooked. Add salt to taste and serve.

Benefits:
This recipe is often used as an adjuvant treatment of disease, i.e. something additional that one consumes to enhance the effectiveness of medical treatment. The porridge if taken regularly works well for constipation, is ideal for obesity and diabetes related problems and is an efficient aid to detoxification of the body system.

Side Effects:
It is advised that those with uric acid and gout problems avoid this porridge as the beans contain purine which is detrimental to them. To counter balance the purine in the beans, serve with plenty of vegetables.

WINTER

MELON
with seaweed porridge

Benincasa hispida (dong gua)

The English term, "winter melon" is a direct translation of the Chinese word for this gourd, dong gua. Winter melons have featured in Chinese cuisine for thousands of years, with the earliest mention dating from the 2nd century A.D. Mild and sweet in flavour, they are cultivated all over China but there are claims that the best winter melons come from the regions around Guangzhou as well as the best recipes for cooking them! Winter melons have always been food and medicine in Chinese history.

Ingredients:

100g winter melon
30g barley
30g red beans

30g dried seaweed (kelp)
1 litre water
salt to taste with a pinch of brown sugar

Method:

1) Carefully cut away the hard rind of the winter melon. Remove the pulp and seeds. Rinse and cut the flesh into cubes.
2) Soak the dried seaweed in water for 3 hours. Wash, rinse and slice into bite sized pieces.
3) Wash the red beans and barley. Drain.
4) Place all the ingredients except the sugar in a pot. Add water. Cook until porridge consistency. When the winter melon cubes are soft and thoroughly cooked, add the salt and sugar and serve.

Benefits:

In Chinese medical terms, winter melon porridge helps to improve spleen functions, acts as a diuretic, lower blood pressure, reduce fats in the blood and prevent cancer. The dish reduces gall tumours, lowers high cholesterol and prevents goitre. It is also used to treat mycobacterium scrofulaceum. It is believed to suppress hunger and reduce body weight, making it a good choice for anyone on a diet.

Side Effects:

There are no known side effects to consuming winter melons.

THE DHARMA
of a Vegetarian diet

"Nothing will benefit human health and increase chances of survival for life on earth as much as the evolution to a vegetarian diet." - Albert Einstein

While Buddhism is not the only religion that advocates "do not kill", it may be the most prevalent. Compassion is the very heart of Buddhism and it applies to all sentient beings. This includes recognising and respecting that all creatures, great or small, do not wish to suffer and feel pain. There are many today who embrace vegetarianism simply because of this motivation.

It is important to note that the Buddha did not forbid his disciples from eating meat. The only prohibition was that they did not eat meat if the animal was expressly killed for them. As such, monks from certain schools including the Theravada school, do not reject meat which is offered to them when they are on their alms rounds.

Whether it is due to tradition or habituation, many people do perceive becoming a vegetarian as painfully hard or even absurd. However, by allowing one's mind and choices to change one day at a time, we will see amazing results. It may not happen overnight, but it will definitely happen over time. Hence, vegetarianism is really a journey about changing how we live and think.

The best way to start this journey of loving kindness is to acquire more information and knowledge on the value of vegetarianism. It is all about making the informed conscientious choice.

Does Vegetarianism Meet All Nutritional Needs?
Most certainly. Plants, seeds, fruits, nuts, legumes and dairy products are good sources of protein, essential and non-essential amino acids, vitamins and minerals including calcium, iron and zinc. The specially selected vegetables and other ingredients in this book are filled with nutrients. They are low in fat, but rich

in fiber, folic acid, vitamin C and minerals like calcium and magnesium which is required in maintaining a healthy body. They also contain phyto-chemicals which boost the body's immune system, and in repairing of cells.

Most vegetarian diets are generally lower in total fat, saturated fat and cholesterol when compared to the diets of non-vegetarians. Some studies indicate that vegetarians seem to have a lower risk of obesity, coronary heart disease, hypertension (high blood pressure), diabetes mellitus and some forms of cancer.

Some vegetarians, however, do consume eggs. In fact, three of the recipes in this book include eggs. Eggs that are free-range are most preferred, and not from battery hens. Battery hens are subject to very harsh living conditions whereby they cannot even spread their wings or ever see daylight. They are fed various types of growth hormones and antibiotics in order to expedite egg 'production'. We do not recommend using or consuming eggs 'produced' under such conditions.

The recipes in this book combine the ancient healing methods of traditional Chinese medicine with the nutritional benefits of vegetarianism, which provides intrinsic healing to the body and spirit. The benefits are not only for our health but also enrich our humanity. This is the dharma of a vegetarian diet. It is the new health mantra for today's lifestlye.

"Our task must be to free ourselves... by widening our circle of compassion to embrace all living creatures and the whole of nature and its beauty. " - Albert Einstein

TOMATO

AND ONION
scrambled omelette

Lycopersicum esculentum (fan qie)

The tomato is native to South and Central America. The Aztecs cultivated them and gave them the name, xitomatl. The Spanish conquerors took them to Europe where they became popular. It is believed that Christian missionaries took them to China in the 16th century. In Chinese medicine, the tomato is said to help with spleen, liver and kidney functions. Indeed, one remedy for hangovers is said to be tomato juice!

Ingredients:

4 medium tomatoes roughly diced
1 medium red onion diced
5 free range eggs whisked well
salt to taste with a pinch of brown sugar

4 tbsp vegetable oil
2 cloves garlic finely chopped
2 inch ginger thinly sliced

Method:

1) Heat 2 tablespoons of oil in a pan. Add the whisked eggs. Scramble till just set. Remove and set aside.
2) Add the remaining oil to the pan. Add onion, ginger, garlic and sauté until fragrant. Add tomatoes and stir fry for a few seconds. Then add the scrambled eggs and mix well.
3) When tomatoes are cooked but still a little firm, add in a bit of salt to taste and a pinch of brown sugar. Serve piping hot.

Benefits:

Tomatoes are thirst quenchers, nourishing the stomach and digestive system. Many nutritionists use tomatoes to treat fever, bleeding gums, anaemia, dizziness, palpitations, hypertension, night blindness and myopia. It is also recommended for acute and chronic hepatitis and nephritis. Among the vegetables that fight and prevent cancer, tomatoes are ranked among the top ten!

Side effects:

There are no known side effects found in tomatoes.

PUMPKIN

PANFRIED
in sweet egg batter

Cucurbita spp (nan gua)

Pumpkins, fat and fleshy, complete with vines and leaves have traditionally featured in Chinese art and carvings, symbolising fertility and abundance. Nothing left to waste, all parts of the pumpkin that are not eaten are given to livestock to feed. In Chinese traditional medicine, the pumpkin as well as its seeds (nan gua zi) are used to alleviate various health problems.

Ingredients:

500g pumpkin thickly sliced
50g unbleached flour
2 free range eggs

1 tbsp sugar
5 tbsp vegetable oil
generous pinch of salt

Method:

1) Break the 2 eggs in a bowl. Whisk lightly. Keep aside.
2) In another bowl, blend the flour with sugar and salt. Make a well in the middle and add the whisked eggs. Mix thoroughly, adding water bit by bit to make a thick paste.
3) Dip pumpkin slices into this mixture and make sure to coat well.
4) Heat the oil in a non stick pan. Pan-fry the coated pumpkin slices. Remove when golden brown. Drain on paper towels. Serve hot.

Benefits:

Pumpkins are neutral in constitution. They are used in remedies for cough and asthma as well as to improve lung functions as they help discharge mucus. They are also used for detoxification and as parasite cleanser for the digestive system. Pumpkins help lower blood sugar, clear heavy metals in the body and are great thirst quenchers! For those with diabetic, hypertension and constipation problems, pumpkins should be a perfect vegetable of choice!

Side effects:

Pumpkins can cause heatiness in the body apart from diarrhoea. They are not suitable for people with hyper sensitive skin.

DUMPLINGS

WITH chives and egg filling

Allium schoenoprasum (jiao zi)

Dumplings have been part of Chinese cuisine for over 1000 years. Apparently, a wooden bowl of dumplings was found in a Tang dynasty tomb in Turpan. Shaped like ancient gold ingots, dumplings are traditionally eaten during Chinese New Year by the whole family to usher in good luck. Nowadays though, dumplings are eaten all year round.

Ingredients:

300g chives finely chopped
4 free range eggs scrambled
1 inch ginger finely chopped
2 tbsp soy sauce
2 tbsp vegetable oil

1 star anise
1 tbsp Sichuan pepper
1 ½ cup unbleached flour
½ cup water (room temperature)
salt to taste with a pinch of brown sugar

Method:

1) In a bowl, combine the chives, eggs, ginger, soy sauce, salt and sugar. Mix well.
2) Heat the vegetable oil in a pan. Sauté the star anise and Sichuan pepper till fragrant then discard. Quickly add the egg and chives mixture and stir well. Leave aside to cool.
3) Sift the flour in a bowl. Add water and knead till the dough is smooth. Add more flour (or water) as required. Roll the dough into little balls measuring about 1 inch in diameter. Flatten with a rolling pin into a circle of 4 inches in diameter.
4) Place a tablespoon of the filling in the centre of the circle. Fold into half. Crimp the edges of the semi-circle (using your index finger and thumb) and tightly seal the dumpling. Gently drop the dumplings into a pot of boiling water. The moment the dumplings float to the surface, they can be removed and served.

Benefits:

Chives are warm in constitution. It is believed they nourish the kidney, liver and stomach. They function as laxatives as well.

Side effects:

There are no side effects. However, those who practise Zen meditation should not consume chives frequently as they increase the male libido.

Acknowledgements:

We would like to firstly express our deepest gratitude to our Spiritual Guide H. E. Tsem Tulku Rinpoche for his inspiration and guidance on this cookbook. It was Tsem Tulku Rinpoche who initiated the idea for this book because Rinpoche's health improved with Dr. Jiang's recipes and treatments. As a result, His Eminence wishes to share the goodness of healthy recipes with everyone.

Special Appreciation:

This book would not be possible without the main sponsorship of kind individuals whom we would like to especially mention:

Dato' Tony Tan, D.I.M.P.

Mr. William Man

Also, thank you to:

Dato' Ruby Khong, D.I.M.P.
Mr. Jeff Ong
Mdm. Foon Foon Kooi
Mr. Wan Wai Meng
Mr. Stanislav Bologov
Mr. Alvyn Lee and Ms. Sherry Low

KECHARA

Established in 2000, Kechara is a non-profit Buddhist organisation under the spiritual guidance of His Eminence Tsem Tulku Rinpoche. It is an affiliate of the illustrious 600-year-old Gaden Shartse Monastery, which is now situated in Mundgod, South India. Gaden Shartse Monastery belongs to the holy Gaden Monastery which now houses more than 3,000 monks and is regarded as one of the most elite monastic universities in the world.

The Kechara organisation seeks to bring the beautiful, ancient wisdom of Buddhism to as many people as possible around the world. It offers a range of programmes that include introductory classes on Buddhism, prayer sessions and wonderful opportunities to volunteer in Buddhist-related arts, publishing and community service.

While based in Malaysia and Nepal, Kechara also has supporters and friends from all around the world who follow its activities via its website and online social network. Since its inception, Kechara has grown into several departments:

Tsem Ladrang
The private residence and office of H.E. Tsem Tulku Rinpoche; also the headquarters of the Kechara organisation.

Kechara House
The main Dharma centre which is based on the outskirts of Kuala Lumpur, Malaysia.

Kechara Animal Sanctuary
A community project dedicated to rescuing and providing relief to abused and abandoned animals.

Kechara Care
An information and visitors' centre for the organisation.

Kechara Discovery
A travel consultancy which organises pilgrimages to holy places and sources for statues to complement the selection at the outlets.

Kechara InMotion
A film production house.

Kechara Lounge
An information centre and lounge overlooking the Boudhanath Stupa in Kathmandu, Nepal.

Kechara Media & Publications
The publishing arm.

Kechara Oasis
A new-age vegetarian restaurant.

Kechara Paradise
Retail outlets in prominent areas of Kuala Lumpur and Penang, offering handicrafts and artifacts from the Himalayan region.

Kechara Saraswati Arts
The first Himalayan arts studio in Southeast Asia.

Kechara Soup Kitchen
A community action group which distributes food to the homeless and urban poor in Malaysia.

Kechara World Peace Centre
The future spiritual sanctuary and alternative arts, healing and philosophy centre in Malaysia

If you would like to know more about Kechara, please contact us at:

Kechara House
No 7, Jalan PJU 1/3G,
SunwayMas Commercial Centre,
47301 Petaling Jaya,
Selangor, Malaysia

Tel   : (+603) 7803 3908
Fax   : (+603) 7803 3108
E-mail : care@kechara.com
Website : www.kechara.com

KECHARA MEDIA & PUBLICATIONS

Kechara Media & Publications (KMP) is a not-for-profit publishing arm of the Kechara Buddhist Organisation. First established in 2005 by a group of young and dedicated students, KMP's vision is to bring H.E. Tsem Tulku Rinpoche's teachings and the ancient wisdom of Dharma into the context of contemporary living.

KMP also publishes inspirational, motivational books by His Eminence's students, who are talented up-and-coming authors equally committed to bringing this message of peace and wisdom to others. To reach as wide an audience as possible, KMP produces books in English and Chinese that are retailed in the Kechara Dharma stores, leading bookshops and online.

Our work is really a labour of love.

All sponsorships are invaluable to us, as it helps us to continue publishing books that inspire and transform people's minds. We believe that by sponsoring our books, you are directly and actively helping others to connect to this wisdom energy, to gain happiness and peace of mind. You also create the cause to gain tremendous wisdom for yourself, to be able to bring positive change for the betterment of your life and the lives of your loved ones.

By our books, we hope that reading will serve as a powerful and inspiring method for healing and mind transformation – creating a shift from negative ways of thinking, to positive, altruistic and compassionate attitudes. By giving new perspectives and bringing peace through our books, many more people will not only reach out with heartfelt sincerity to help the homeless, abused children and victims of natural disasters but more importantly, be closer, kinder, more compassionate and patient with their families, colleagues, loved ones and society at large. Only through this can we create the causes for Inner Peace and Outer Peace, and eventually World Peace may become a reality.

Thank you for your support of KMP's cause of healing through reading.

For more information about KMP, please contact us at:

Kechara Media & Publications Sdn. Bhd.
41-2A & 41-2B, 1st Floor
Jalan PJU 1/3C
SunwayMas Commercial Centre
47301 Petaling Jaya
Selangor, Malaysia

Tel   : (+603) 7805 5691
Fax   : (+603) 7805 5690
Email   : kmp@kechara.com
Website : www.kechara.com/kmp

We also welcome volunteers to assist with transcribing, translation, editing or graphic design. If you are interested in joining us or in contributing in any way towards the production of books, DVDs and online teachings, please contact us, no matter where you are in the world. We would love to have you on board!

KECHARA WORLD PEACE CENTRE – THE SPIRITUAL HEART OF ASIA

Kechara World Peace Centre (KWPC) is H.E. Tsem Tulku Rinpoche's inspirational vision for the future: a sanctuary for contemplation, education and relaxation. KWPC will be a unique spiritual space in Malaysia for modern people who wish to find peace and happiness.

A unique, all-encompassing destination for anyone from any age to rest, reflect and rejuvenate, KWPC is set amidst the lush and sprawling green foothills of Genting Highlands in Malaysia.

As the cultural and spiritual heart of Asia, KWPC will be an irresistible draw for travellers, the curious and spiritual seekers. It will be a place where anyone can learn and experience aspects of the life and culture of the Himalayas and its ancient, mystical secrets.

Within KWPC, there will be a World Peace hall, a multicultural village, a forest chapel dedicated to Mother Tara, al fresco cafés, meditation chalets, alternative arts and healing therapies, and philosophy classes among many diverse and holistic activities to stimulate the body, speech and mind. KWPC will also address social issues: an old folks home and an animal sanctuary in our efforts to build a better society.

KWPC will be all this and more. Be a part of this inspirational vision. It is your participation and support that will make KWPC a reality.

Join us in creating an incredible legacy for future generations to come.

For more information, visit www.kechara.com/peace-centre
or contact Cheri Woo at tel: (+603) 7880 0189 | email cheri.woo@kechara.com

Kechara World Peace Centre (KWPC) - Scale model of artist impression

GLOSSARY
an introduction to living healthy

The following pages highlight in brief some ailments or diseases that plague humankind which are due, in part, to poor eating habits.

CANCER

In the battle against cancer, scientists are discovering new species of vegetables and plants that are potentially eco-warriors against this dreaded disease. There has been tremendous successful research in this field. Some of the vegetables and plants presented in the recipes of this book have been specially selected for this purpose.

As prevention and fighting cancer works best when medicinal, chemical and dietary treatments are integrated, here are a few dietary tips that can be applied to our daily lives:
- Avoid any kind of dried meat, barbequed or deep fried food.
- Avoid food which is past its expiry date. Always be wise when choosing fresh food.
- Avoid food that is too hot or spicy; reduce the intake of salt; minimize the consumption of pickles and avoid "heaty" food like steamboat soup.
- Avoid constipation. You may end up with a toxic build up in your digestive system if you have irregular bowel movements as your body reabsorbs the toxins, leading to illness.

This book contains a recipe for detox porridge. Not only is this porridge extremely effective in cleansing the body and removing toxins, it is also suggested to help prevent cancer. It is recommended for long term consumption and is suitable for everyone including cancer patients. To add flavour to the porridge, you can add white fungus or wolfberries.

It is best to blanch or quick stir-fry the vegetables or simply serve them as a salad. These are the cooking methods that will lock in the nutrients in the vegetables. Over cooked vegetables lose their nutritious benefits.

Many fruits also contain cancer fighting properties. These include figs, watermelons, papayas, kiwi fruit, lemons and grapes. When it comes to beverages, the best is green tea. Apple cider and juice made from vegetable and fruit enzymes are good too. If you need to sweeten your drinks, substitute refined sugar with honey or agave nectar.

DIABETES

Diabetes is a chronic disease caused by high levels of sugar in the blood. It is one of the most common diseases of modern civilisation. People think that diabetes is caused by over consumption of sugar. This is not true. It comes from consuming too much rich and processed food and not exercising enough. As a result, their surplus energy is not sufficiently metabolised. Over a period of time, this affects the functions of the internal organs, causing metabolic disorder.

We are what we eat, hence diabetes can be treated with the appropriate diet. However, it must be remembered that the process of nourishing internal organs back to health is a long one. Recovery takes time. Chances of recovery are higher if we know how to avoid further damage to our internal organs. Diabetes may not be caused by excess consumption of sugar; nevertheless, too much consumption of sugar and refined carbohydrates does not help. The same goes for the consumption of fruits that have high sugar content.

Other than sweet potatoes, the vegetables listed in the recipes are all low in sugar and calories. They will not damage internal organs and are suitable for long term consumption.

Fruits must be consumed in moderation because some have higher sugar content than others. These include red dates, bananas, grapes, longans, mandarin oranges and mangoes. For long term consumption, select fruits that contain comparatively less sugar such as pomeloes, pineapples, strawberries, peaches, lemons, cherries and plums.

EXCESSIVE BODY WEIGHT

The fundamental cause of excessive weight is an energy imbalance, i.e. there is more energy intake as food than energy output as physical activity and basal metabolic needs. Therefore, the excess intake is stored in the body as fat.

Can you really lose weight effectively by eating less? The truth is you can't! An effective diet plan should not require you to starve. It should use natural food sources and their functions to improve and boost metabolism. When the right kind of food is selected and matched with balanced intake, the function of natural food becomes far more effective than any detox or weight loss medicine.

Tips for losing weight:

- *Avoid consuming cold drinks:* The sudden intake of cold drinks obstructs the regular circulation of qi and blood in the human body. As a result the metabolism rate will decrease tremendously. Subsequently, the process of fat burning also slows down or ceases completely. In healthy bodies, it takes at least an hour to return to the previous normal state. For those whose health is frail, it takes even longer to recover.
- *Avoid eating 4 hours before sleep:* If you eat before bedtime, the digestive system stays awake to digest the food while you sleep. Instead of regular circulation in the body, most of the blood will be diverted to your digestive tract, causing microcirculatory impairment in other organs. This slows down metabolism. Eventually, this increases fat storage in the body.
- *Avoid drinking coffee:* Caffeine in coffee increases the level of free fatty acids in blood plasma in which triglycerides are present. To make matters worse, we love to add sugar in our coffee. We might as well add flavour to our body fat.
- *Avoid consuming sugary drinks:* Over consumption of sugar leads to weight gain. Try to minimize the intake of sugar in all drinks. A better alternative is to replace sugar with honey.
- *Avoid skipping meals:* You may think skipping meals is the best way to lose weight. Initially, this may appear true. You may actually lose weight but due to excess energy expenditure, the chances of gaining more weight after you resume eating will be much higher.

CONSTIPATION

Constipation, which is caused by irregular bowel movement, results in the body storing and absorbing toxic substances. It causes more than 30 kinds of diseases and health problems. Some of the more common ones are liver disease, colon cancer, hemorrhoids, high blood pressure, headaches, skin diseases, bad breath and obesity. Constipation is largely due to unhealthy eating habits.

Fruits such as dragon fruits, papayas, apples, grapes, oranges, bananas and pineapples are excellent choices that help relieve constipation. Select any or mix the fruits as you wish and consume daily.

减重贴士：
- 严忌冷饮：人体的气血正在规律的运行，突然摄入冰饮，只会导致新陈代谢立刻减缓，代谢过程中的脂肪燃烧也会减缓动作，甚至完全停止运作。身体健康较好的人要一小时左右后才能恢复自然状态；身体虚弱者则需要较长的时间恢复。

- 睡前4小时忌食：若在睡前进食即表示肠胃在睡眠时仍处于活跃状态。因此大量的血液流向消化道，导致分布在其他器官的血液相对减少，形成微循环障碍，直接影响人体新陈代谢的速度。日子久了，脂肪滞留，肥胖就找上门来了。

- 忌饮用咖啡：咖啡因会使血液中的游离脂肪酸升高，而游离脂肪酸就是甘油三酯的基础；加上我们一般喝咖啡时喜欢加糖，这无形中就为肥胖多加了一份调味料。

- 忌饮用含糖份饮品：过量的摄入糖份会造成肥胖。喝饮品时尽量将糖份减至最低；若不习惯，可以尝试用蜂蜜代替白糖。

- 断食非正确选择：一般人认为断食是减肥的最佳方法；一开始体重会减轻，但因为过度耗损热量，一旦恢复饮食，体重增加的机率会高出更多。

便秘

便秘是肠蠕动不寻常的结果，也导致排泄物滞留在体内并累积更多的毒素。超过30种疾病和健康问题的缘由皆因便秘。其中较为普遍的疾病包括肝病、结肠癌、痔疮、高血压、头痛、皮肤问题、口臭和肥胖等问题。大部分的便秘问题是因饮食不均衡导致。

火龙果、木瓜、苹果、葡萄、橙、香蕉和黄梨都是治疗便秘的最佳水果。你每天可以依个人喜好选择以上一种或将多种水果混合食用。

糖尿病

糖尿病是一种因血液里糖份过高导致的慢性疾病，更是现代文明病之一。一般上我们都认为糖尿病是因为平时饮食中摄取过量的糖份才会引起，其实这是错误的观念。在中国传统医术的角度，糖尿病也被称为消渴病，或是富贵病。那是因为糖尿病患者大多来自富有人家，美食吃多了，但却没有适量的运动，导致剩余的热量没有充分的被分解。日子久了，就会影响内脏的运作，导致新陈代谢失常。

古人曰："病从口入"，所以糖尿病是可以通过饮食调节医治。但要让内脏恢复正常运作，并非是一朝一夕的事。事实上只要不让受损的内脏受到更严重的伤害，那修复的机会就会就更高了。虽然糖尿病不是因为糖份摄取过量造成，但摄入过量的糖份或精细碳水化合物始终对健康无益。同样地，高糖量的水果类也要做适当的摄取。

菜类中除了番薯外，其余的都是低糖与低热量，不用担心会伤害脏腑，更可以长期食用。

水果类也必须适量食用，因为一些水果的含糖量比其他水果高出许多，如红枣、香蕉、葡萄、龙眼、芦柑、芒果等。若想长期食用，可选择含糖量较低的水果如：黄瓜、西瓜、柚子、黄梨、草莓、桃、柠檬、樱桃和李子。

肥胖

导致肥胖的主要因素是热量的失衡，好比食用的热量比消耗的热量高出很多，以及多出新陈代谢所需。也因此，多余的热量就会变成脂肪在体内储存。

吃得少就能变瘦吗？其实不然。一个有效的减肥食单是不会让你挨饿，它其实是运用了大自然的食物和其功能，从而改善并促进人体的新陈代谢。选择正确的食材，再摄取适当的份量，排毒减肥药物的效用也不比天然食材来得奏效。

词汇表
活出健康基本知识

接下来的几页将大略解说人类因不良的饮食习惯而患上的疾病。

癌症

在对抗癌症的过程中，科学家发现一些极有潜能对抗那些可怕疾病的蔬菜和植物。目前，这个领域的研究经已获得巨大的成就。一些在这食谱中出现的蔬菜和植物经过特别精选，希望能借此机会让更多的人对抗癌蔬菜和植物有更深的了解。

抵抗癌症的最有效方法便是综合药物、化疗和食疗这三种疗法。以下是你可以在日常生活中实践的饮食贴士：

- 切勿食用烧烤、油炸、腊肉等食品。
- 切勿食用过期食品，力求食材新鲜程度。
- 忌食辛辣刺激性的食物，并减低盐份和腌制品如咸菜的摄取量。至于发热伤阴的食物如火锅的汤底也得减少食用。
- 防止便秘的发生，因为便秘会形成毒素的再吸收，使癌细胞增加养分，让病情恶化。

此书为读者提供排毒粥的食谱。排毒粥不但具有排毒作用，更具有抗癌、防癌的作用。除了癌症患者，其他人也可以将排毒粥当作主食长期食用。你可以在粥中添加银耳或枸杞子以让味道更为丰富。

将蔬菜氽烫和清炒，或者弄成沙拉是烹调蔬菜的最佳选择。因为这些烹调方法能有效锁住蔬菜内的营养成分；长时间的炖煮，只会使大部分的养分流失。

无花果、西瓜、木瓜、奇异果、柠檬和葡萄都是具抗癌效用的水果。至于抗癌饮品，绿茶就是最佳的选择。苹果酒或蔬菜和水果类酵素都是很好的抗癌饮料。而日常食用的糖类，可以用蜂蜜或者龙舌兰花蜜代替白糖。

克切拉世界和平中心——亚洲的灵修圣地

克切拉世界和平中心（KWPC）是尊贵的詹杜固仁波切的愿景：一个结合了禅修、教育及休闲的圣地。它将成为马来西亚境内一所适合现代人追寻宁静与快乐的理想之地。

位于云顶山脚下的克切拉世界和平中心，伫立在一片青山绿野之间，是一个适合所有年龄层人士前来休息与充电的独特所在。

作为亚洲的文化与灵修圣地，克切拉世界和平中心将对游客及心灵探索者，形成一股不可抗拒的魅力。在这里，每个人都可学习和体验喜马拉雅山的习俗及文化，并探索其古老而神秘的色彩。

在克切拉世界和平中心内，将建有世界和平厅、多元文化村、森林度母殿、露天咖啡馆、禅修小舍，并设有另类艺术及疗法和哲学课程等，旨在透过多元化的身心灵活动，净化我们的身语意，从而提升我们的心灵层次。此外，为了推动社会关怀服务，克切拉世界和平中心内也将设有安老院及动物庇护所，为创建一个更美好的社会献一份力。

克切拉世界和平中心将不止如此。请加入我们，成为共同实现这个愿景的一份子。你的参与和支持，将让克切拉世界和平中心成为一个现实。

现在就加入我们的团队，让我们携手为未来的世代，创造一个不朽的传世净土。

欲知详情，请浏览www.kechara.com/peace-centre，
或联络胡淑燕（Cheri Woo）电话：+603 7880 0189；
电邮：cheri.woo@kechara.com

克切拉世界和平中心（KWPC）——画家眼中的缩小图

克切拉媒体出版社

克切拉媒体出版社是一家隶属于克切拉团体的非营利出版社。它成立于2005年,由尊贵的詹杜固仁波切一群热诚十足的学生所创办。出版社的愿景,是希望能将詹仁波切的法教及古老的佛法智慧带入现代人的生活。

克切拉媒体出版社也出版仁波切学生们所编写的激励性与启发性的书籍。这些极具天分的作者亦追随仁波切的步伐,矢志把和平与智慧的讯息带给大家。为了让更多人能接触到我们的书籍,除了克切拉佛教文物中心之外,克切拉媒体出版社所出版的中英文书籍也在各大书局及网上发售。

我们的工作是由爱心砌成的

每一位赞助者的帮助对我们来说都是很珍贵的,有了他们的支持,我们才得以继续出版能启发人心及转化思维的书籍。我们相信,透过赞助我们的书籍,你们不但直接协助他人与这个智慧能量做连接,同时也帮助他们获得一颗快乐及平静的心。此外,你为自己种下的善因,除了有助于让你在未来能取得大量的智慧之外,也让你及所爱的人获得更好的生活。

我们希望藉由我们的书籍,让阅读成为一个疗愈心灵及促进心灵转化的有效方式,并把负面思维转化为正面、利他及慈悲的态度。透过我们文字传达的崭新角度及和平讯息,许多人将会以真诚的心去协助无家可归者、受虐儿童及天灾灾黎,而更重要的是,他们将对自己的家人、同事、心爱的人及整个社会投以更多的善心、爱心和耐心,拉近人与人之间的距离。只有这样,我们才能为取得内、外在的宁静种下善因,继而世界和平中心才会有实现的一天。

感谢您支持克切拉媒体出版社"透过阅读种下疗愈之因"的努力。

欲知有关克切拉媒体出版社详情,请联络:

克切拉媒体出版社有限公司
41-2A & 41-2B, 1st Floor
Jalan PJU 1/3C
SunwayMas Commercial Centre
47301 Petaling Jaya
Selangor, Malaysia

电话:(+603) 7805 5691
传真:(+603) 7805 5690
电邮:kmp@kechara.com
网站:kechara.com/kmp

我们也诚邀志愿工作者协助我们进行听写、翻译、编辑及平面设计工作。如果您有意加入我们,或想透过其他任何方式支持我们出版各类书籍、影音光碟或网上教材,请联络我们。无论您身在何处,我们都无任欢迎您的加入!

克切拉团体

克切拉团体是一个成立于公元2000年的非盈利佛教团体。它附属于拥有600年辉煌历史的甘丹萨济寺,以尊贵的詹杜固仁波切作为其精神导师。目前位于印度孟过的甘丹萨济寺隶属拥有3,000名僧人的甘丹寺,是世界上最著名的佛教学院之一。

克切拉团体的成立,旨在将古老美丽的佛教智慧,带给世界上许许多多的人。其所举办的一系列活动,包括佛学入门班、法会,以及为志愿者提供参与佛教艺术、出版以及社会服务工作的机会。

尽管克切拉团体的主要据点设于马来西亚和尼泊尔,它目前也拥有来自全球各地的朋友和支持者。他们多透过网站和与时俱进的各种互联网及社交网络服务来追随克切拉的各种活动。自成立以来,克切拉已经扩展至多个不同的部门:

詹拉章	:尊贵的詹杜固仁波切之私人居所及办公处,也是克切拉团体的总部。
克切拉佛教中心	:位于马来西亚吉隆坡市郊的佛教中心。
克切拉动物庇护所	:矢志拯救遭虐待及被遗弃动物的社区计划。
克切拉亲善部	:克切拉团体的访客及咨询中心。
克切拉新纪元	:专组办朝圣团的旅游咨询中心,同时也负责寻觅适合的佛像,为文物中心增添更丰富多元的佛像系列。
克切拉映像制作	:专业影像制作公司。
克切拉自在坊	:克切拉团体设于尼泊尔加德满都博达哈大佛塔附近的咨询中心。
克切拉媒体出版社	:克切拉团体的出版臂膀。
克切拉如意轩	:新时代素食馆。
克切拉天堂	:位于吉隆坡及槟城市区的佛教文物中心,专提供来自喜马拉雅地区的手工艺品。
克切拉妙音艺术坊	:东南亚第一间喜马拉雅艺术工作坊。
克切拉香积厨	:为马来西亚的无家可归者及都市贫穷户分派食物的社区活动小组。
克切拉世界和平中心	:马来西亚未来的心灵庇护所和另类艺术、治疗及哲学中心。

欲了解更多有关克切拉团体的详情,请联络我们:

克切拉佛教中心
No 7, Jalan PJU 1/3G,
SunwayMas Commercial Centre,
47301 Petaling Jaya,
Selangor, Malaysia.

电话: (+603) 7803 3908
传真: (+603) 7803 3108
电邮: care@kechara.com
网站: www.kechara.com

鸣谢

在此,我们首先要向我们的精神导师尊贵的詹杜固仁波切致上万分谢意。没有他的启发和指导,就不会有今天这本食谱。这本食谱的出版是詹杜固仁波切的主意,因为他的健康状况在经过姜医师的食疗配方和医治后改善许多。因此,詹杜固仁波切希望能将这利于众人的健康食谱与每一个人分享。

特别感谢

感谢以下热心人士的赞助,这食谱才得以顺利出版。

Dato' Tony Tan, D.I.M.P.

Mr. William Man

与此同时,我们也想向以下人士致以谢意。

Dato' Ruby Khong, D.I.M.P.
Mr. Jeff Ong
Mdm Foon Foon Kooi
Mr. Wan Wai Meng
Mr. Stanislav Bologov
Mr. Alvyn and Ms Sherry Low

水

饺

饺子

超过千多年来，水饺都不曾从中国美食单中缺席。水饺在吐鲁番市唐朝陵墓中的一木制碗中被发现。水饺的形状仿似中国古时候的金元宝，传统上人们一般会在农历新年期间食用以表示迎接好运气。如今人们都常年食用水饺。

材料：

韭菜切碎	300克	八角	1朵
放养鸡蛋（炒蛋）	4颗	花椒	1汤匙
姜切碎	1寸	未漂白面粉	1 ½ 杯
生抽	2汤匙	水（室温）	½杯
植物油	2汤匙	盐和红糖	适量

方法：

1) 将韭菜、鸡蛋、姜、生抽、盐和红糖放入碗中搅拌均匀。
2) 再将植物油倒入锅中待热，再放入八角和花椒爆香直至香味传出。后将八角和花椒弃掉，并快速地将混合物倒入锅中再与热油搅拌均匀。暂置一旁待冷却。
3) 制作水饺皮的方法：面粉筛入碗中，再加入水和面粉混合擀匀直至面团表面平滑（如有需要可以自加面粉和水），再分割成横径一寸大小的小面团。以擀面棍压平，并擀成横径四寸左右的面皮。
4) 取一汤匙馅料，置入水饺皮中央，将之对折。用拇指和食指将水饺皮封口。接着将水饺放入滚水中直至水饺浮上水面。最后取出水饺即可上桌。

功效：

韭菜性质温和，能滋养肾、肝和胃，同时也有助于通便。

缺点：

没有任何缺点。只是禅修者不宜多食，因为韭菜具刺激性欲的作用。

炸

南瓜

南瓜
南瓜身形大而丰满，它的藤和叶子在中国传统雕刻和艺术上有崇高的地位，更象征着肥沃和丰裕。南瓜的每个部位都被充份的使用，就算是不能食用的部位也能用以喂食家畜。在中国传统医术上，南瓜和其种子（南瓜子）拥有减轻各种健康问题的功效。

材料：

南瓜切成厚片	500克	红糖	1汤匙
未漂白面粉	50克	植物油	5汤匙
放养鸡蛋	2颗	盐	适量

方法：
1) 将2颗放养鸡蛋打入碗中搅拌后暂置一旁。
2) 在另一碗中将面粉、红糖和盐混合，并在混合物中间留一个空洞以倒入搅拌后的鸡蛋。随后再搅拌均匀，慢慢倒入水以弄成糊状。
3) 将切成厚片的南瓜蘸入混合物中并确保南瓜片完全被包覆。
4) 在不沾锅中倒入植物油待热后将南瓜片炸直至呈金黄色。最后将炸好的南瓜片置在放着纸巾的盘上以吸走多余的油量。建议趁热食用。

功效：
南瓜性质属微温，除了能润肺益气、止咳平喘去痰、解毒驱虫外，也有助降低血糖、止渴、清除体内重金属。南瓜食疗更是高血压、便秘、糖尿病患者的首选。

缺点：
南瓜容易产生湿热，同时患有皮肤瘙痒者忌食。

蕃茄

炒蛋

蕃茄

番茄源自于南美洲和中美洲。它是由阿兹台克人种植并取名为"xitomatl"。后来西班牙人将番茄带到欧洲——一个让番茄闻名的地方。据说基督教传教士在16世纪时把番茄带到中国。而在中国传统医术里，番茄有着加强脾、肝和肾在体内运作的功效。事实上，番茄汁被认为是宿醉的"解药"。

材料：

番茄切块	4颗（中等大小）	植物油	4汤匙
洋葱切半再切块	1颗（中等大小）	蒜头切碎	2瓣
放养鸡蛋	5粒（打散）	姜片切薄	2寸
盐和红糖	适量		

方法：

1) 将2汤匙的植物油倒入锅中待热，再放入鸡蛋炒至成形。随后将成形的鸡蛋取出并暂置一旁。
2) 接着再将剩余的植物油倒入锅中待热。加入洋葱、蒜头和姜爆香直至香味传出。之后放入番茄翻炒数秒再放入鸡蛋搅和。
3) 在番茄煮熟但还没完全煮软时加入适量的盐和红糖即可。在热腾腾的时候食用最佳。

功效：

番茄一直都被认为能生津止渴、健胃消食。大部分医师都用番茄来改善发热、牙龈出血、贫血、头晕、心悸、高血压、急慢性肝炎、急慢性肾炎、夜盲症和近视眼的问题。在抗癌蔬菜里，番茄排在前十名内。

缺点：

无明显缺点。

素食相较于荤食所摄取的总脂肪量、饱和脂肪以及胆固醇量都来得低。更有一些研究指出素食者罹患肥胖、冠心病、高血压、糖尿病和其他癌症的机率比一般人来得低。

一些素食者也食用鸡蛋。事实上，本书食谱中也有三道菜是以蛋为材料。当然放养鸡所下的蛋是最佳的选择，而并非格子笼母鸡所下的蛋。这是因为格子笼里的母鸡生存在恶劣的环境中。它们从来无法展翅，更从不见天日。它们被喂以多种生长激素和抗生素，以促进母鸡下蛋的数量。我们不建议大家食用这种在"强迫行为"底下生产的鸡蛋。

这本食谱结合中国古代的治疗方法和素食的营养好处，为身和心带来本质性的治疗。这不止为我们的身体健康带来好处，更丰富了我们的慈悲心。这就是素食的佛法，也是现代生活方式的保健心咒。

"我们的任务必须是解放自己……扩大我们的慈悲以拥抱所有生命和大自然的美。" – 爱因斯坦

素食中的
佛法

"没有任何东西能比成为素食者更有利于人们提升自身的健康,同时也提高其他生物的生存机会。" - 爱因斯坦

佛教并不是唯一主张不杀生的宗教,但却最提倡不杀生。对众生怀慈悲心乃是佛教的中心思想,这其中包括了对每个生物的认可和尊重,无论那生物有多巨大或多细小,都不忍它们痛苦。现今亦有不少人因为这众生平等的动机而奉行素食主义。

我们必须清楚知道,佛陀并没有禁止他的弟子吃肉。唯一的严禁是动物不能为了成为他们的盘中餐而牺牲。正因如此,南传佛教的僧侣在化缘时才不会拒绝他人布施的荤食。

无论是基于传统或习惯的缘由,很多人认为成为素食者是艰难的,甚至是荒谬至极的事。但是,当一个人在某个时间点上转念及改变自己的选择,我们会看见让人赞叹的结果。结果当然不会在明天就实现,但总有成真的一天。因此,素食主义是一段人们生活和思维转变的征途。

开始这段慈悲征途的最好方法,便是了解素食主义价值的资讯和知识。这是为了在做出认真的选择前,了解得更透彻。

素食主义能获取所有的营养所需吗?
当然可以。蔬菜、种子、水果、坚果、豆类和乳制品都是绝佳的蛋白质、必需和非必需氨基酸、维他命和矿物质如钙、铁和锌的来源。食谱中特别精选的蔬菜和食材都是营养成分极高的材料。那些食材不仅脂肪含量低,更具备了维持人体健康所需的高纤维、叶酸、维他命C、钙和镁。那些食材也含有提升人体免疫系统及修复细胞作用的植物化学物质。

利水

冬瓜粥

冬瓜的英文名字"winter melon"是中文"冬瓜"的直译。在中国美食中，冬瓜自上千年来一直扮演重要的角色，而最早被记载用以料理中是在公元二世纪。冬瓜肉柔软香甜，在中国各地都可以找到冬瓜的种植地；但有人声称广州地区的冬瓜质量和其烹饪法是最为出色的。冬瓜在中国历史上一直是食品，更常被用在医药上。

材料：

冬瓜	100克	干海带	30克
薏米	30克	水	1公升
红豆	30克	盐和红糖	适量

方法：
1) 削去冬瓜皮，再将种子去掉。随后将果肉洗净并切成块状。
2) 将干海带浸入水中3小时，再洗净并切成小片状。
3) 洗净红豆和薏米，沥干。
4) 将所有的材料放入锅中（红糖除外），再倒入水。煮至粥绵滑后确保冬瓜肉已经软化并经已煮熟。最后加入适量的盐和红糖即可。

功效：
中国传统医术上，此料理能产生健脾利水，降血压、血脂及防癌的效用。同时也适用于瘿瘤（大颈包）、瘰疬、高胆固醇及预防甲状腺肿大或癌变的疾病。冬瓜对于减肥也有相当不错的效果。

缺点：
无明显缺点。

排毒

粥

神农氏是中国历史中的传奇人物。他在公元前2853年宣布五谷：稻、小麦、粟、薏米和黄豆，为至高无上的谷物。薏米是绝佳的食物纤维来源，具有降火、排毒以及健脾的功效。黄豆则有在中国种植超过5000年的历史，也具降火的功效，同时更是蛋白质的绝佳来源。除此，黄豆也能清毒润肺以及肠。黑豆、绿豆以及红豆则是菜豆的一种。它们都富有纤维、蛋白质、矿物质、维他命，更有抗氧的功效。

材料：

黑豆	20克	薏米	40克
黄豆	20克	番薯	200克
绿豆	40克	水	1公升
红豆	40克	盐	适量

方法：
1) 在未煮前先把所有的豆粒和薏米洗净并浸入水中（水面得覆盖豆粒和薏米）30分钟。随后沥干并暂置一旁。
2) 将番薯削皮，洗净并切成块状。
3) 将所有材料放入锅中，并倒入水直至覆盖材料。待热滚后将火关小。随后用小火慢煮，直至所有材料熟透。加入适量的盐后即可食用。

功效：
此料理经常被当成治疗疾病的辅助食品。尤其用以治疗便秘最见效。长期食用排毒效果非常明显，也特别适合肥胖和糖尿病人。

缺点：
豆类含有嘌呤，故此尿酸痛风的病人不宜食用。配合大量蔬菜食用，有助于清除豆类嘌呤的作用。

忘忧

金针菜

数个世纪以来,以花蕾为材料的中国美食并不少见。金针菜亦属花蕾的一种,中国人常将之使用在膳食和药物中。金针菜也被称为"金针",其寿命仅有一天之长,所以这道汤才有了"忘忧"这个名字。当金针菜长三至五寸长并开始干化时便可以收割。金针菜在干化时会呈金黄色。未煮前在金针菜的中间打个结更能将金针菜的味道带出。

材料:

金针菜	1杯	姜片切薄	1寸
竹笋切片	1杯	糙米醋	3茶匙
干香菇切片	3朵	盐	1茶匙
银耳	50克	玉米粉	3茶匙
酸枣仁	20克	黑胡椒	1茶匙
粉丝	50克	蔬菜高汤	1公升
盐和红糖	适量		

方法:

1) 将1杯水倒入锅中煮滚,再将酸枣仁放入水中熬20分钟。随后将籽去掉并将熬好的汤暂置一旁。
2) 之后再把香菇、粉丝和金针菜各别分开浸入热水直至软化。沥干后暂置一旁。去除银耳的梗,再浸入热水中直至颜色转淡。随后洗净并沥干。
3) 再将全部材料(玉米粉除外)放入大锅中煮30分钟。将一点水参入玉米粉中搅拌成糊状再倒入汤中。搅拌均匀后即可上桌。

功效:

金针菜性质平和,具有养血平肝、利尿消肿、补脑安神的效用。同时也用于头晕耳鸣,失眠心悸。在中国传统医术上金针菜乃是补脑圣品。

缺点:

含有秋水仙碱,是一种有毒元素。然而煮透之后,金针菜的毒性就会消失。

安神

银耳羹

银耳
大约200多年前，人们在四川发现野生的银耳（在一些时候它也被称为雪耳）。如今，银耳被种植在中国的山区中。银耳在众多中国草药中扮演重要的角色，更是使肌肤柔软的美容圣物。虽然银耳比黑木耳较甜，然而它们的口感是相同的。银耳在一些时候更被称为"穷人的燕窝"。

材料：
过滤水　　　　300毫升
银耳　　　　　80克
冰糖　　　　　2块(可根据个人口味做调适)
莲子　　　　　10颗

方法：
1) 去除银耳的梗并将它浸入热水中直至银耳呈白色。洗净并沥干。
2) 接着将莲子浸入水中。切记把莲心去掉，因为莲心带有苦味。但是莲心是可以食用的，更可以减少体内的热气。
3) 将所有材料放入一个锅中并煮至沸腾。
4) 沸腾后用小火炖15至20分钟即可。

功效：
性质平和、滋润五脏、益气清肠，是不燥不热的滋补佳品。银耳多糖可以抑制肿瘤的形成，也有对抗放化疗病人副作用的功能。银耳也可用于治疗咳嗽、心悸以及因阴虚体燥而引起的疲惫和失眠，同时亦可提升免疫系统。

缺点：
无明显缺点。

竹笋炒

西兰花

竹笋
中国与竹子的关系必须回溯到古代时期。从食品、寝具和建筑材料,到药物以及作诗的灵感,竹子都与人们的心灵息息相关。松脆细嫩的竹笋几千年以来在中国美食和中国传统医术都占有一席之地。

材料:
竹笋	200克	植物油	3汤匙
西兰花	150克	生抽	2汤匙
洋葱切半再切成4瓣	1颗	盐和红糖	适量
姜片切成薄片	2寸		

方法:
1) 将竹笋浸入滚水2分钟。沥干洗净再切成薄片。如果是罐头竹笋,就将它洗净沥干再暂置一旁。随后将西兰花切成小块再放入滚水中氽烫。沥干后暂置一旁。
2) 将植物油倒入锅中待热,再将姜和洋葱爆香直至香味传出。
3) 放入竹笋片和西兰花翻炒。
4) 最后加入生抽和盐后再翻炒一下。加入适量的糖即可食用。

功效:
竹笋生性微寒,有助于清热化痰、益气和胃。疗效上,能促进肠道蠕动并帮助消化,防止便秘,有益于减肥,更有预防大肠癌的功效。

缺点:
无明显缺点。

海带

炖豆腐

豆腐
豆腐有着深远的历史渊源。淮南王刘安早在公元前164年就发明豆腐这食品。食用豆腐的盛行与李时珍完成其结合中国传统医术，并解释各种动植物、矿物质和其他物品都有其药用价值的《本草纲目》是在同一时期。

材料：
豆腐切成块状	250克	植物油	3汤匙
干海带	20克	八角	3朵
洋葱切半后切成薄片	1颗	过滤水	1.5升
姜片切成薄片	2寸	盐	适量

方法：
1) 将海带浸入水中3小时。洗净并切成小片状。
2) 随后再把豆腐放入滚水中烫1分钟左右以去除杂质。沥干并暂置一旁。
3) 将植物油倒入锅中待热，再加入姜和洋葱爆香直到香味传出。放入海带和豆腐，稍微搅拌。
4) 加入水和八角待沸腾后将火关小。焖30分钟并加入适量的盐即可食用。

功效：
豆腐不含胆固醇，能清热益气、和胃解毒。非常适用于改善高血压、心脏病、动脉硬化、身体燥热，甚至有抗癌的功效。它含有丰富的蛋白质，同时也是非常好的天然补钙剂。

缺点：
不易于消化，脾胃虚弱者不可多食。同时含有不少嘌呤，有痛风者应该少食，并建议与大量绿叶蔬菜搭配食用。

凉拌

菠菜

菠菜

菠菜原产于波斯（伊朗），并拥有另一个名字"aspanakh"。在公元647年，尼泊尔国王将菠菜当作赠品送给中国皇帝，就这样菠菜便在中国留了下来。摩尔人在11世纪将菠菜带到欧洲国家，后来美国著名卡通大力水手更将菠菜的知名度在20世纪孩子群中大大提升。

材料：

菠菜	200克		
蒜头切碎	4瓣	植物油	2汤匙
辣椒粉	1汤匙	糙米醋	1汤匙
花椒	1汤匙	盐和红糖	适量

方法：

1) 将菠菜洗净。随后把菠菜放入滚水中烫30秒，再将菠菜浸入室温的水中。沥干并暂置一旁。
2) 之后将菠菜切成小片状并置入一个碗中。
3) 用糙米粗、盐和红糖调味。
4) 接着开始准备辣椒油。先将植物油倒入锅内待热，再将花椒放入油中爆香直至花椒呈金黄色，随后将花椒取出并弃之。最后将辣椒粉和蒜头加入热油中搅和。
5) 将弄好的辣椒油拌入菠菜后，即可食用。

功效：

菠菜主要能改善高血压、解除便秘问题，同时也能改善贫血和皮肤过敏。糖尿病患者最为适宜食用。

缺点：

菠菜有颇高含量的草酸，而草酸却会影响人体对钙质的吸收，尤其肾病患者，切记少食。解决的方法是千万不要生食，可以用开水稍微烫一下，便可清除大部分的草酸。

清炒

鲍鱼菇

鲍鱼菇
许多世纪以来,在中国、日本、韩国、东欧以及波罗的海国家,蘑菇一直被当作是食疗品。鲍鱼菇是平菇的一种,它质地柔软,形状和味道都与鲍鱼非常相似。

材料:
鲍鱼菇	300克
洋葱切半后切成薄片	1颗
姜片切成薄片	2寸
生抽	1汤匙
植物油	3汤匙
盐和红糖	适量

方法:
1) 在锅里煮水直至水滚后再放入鲍鱼菇。把鲍鱼菇置在滚水中烫两分钟。这样更能带出鲍鱼菇的鲜甜味。随后把鲍鱼菇从锅中拿起并沥干。
2) 接着倒入植物油,待锅热后放入姜和洋葱爆香,直到闻到香味。
3) 随后加入生抽和鲍鱼菇。轻巧地拌炒并加入适量的盐。上桌前再加入红糖即可。

功效:
人们一直以来深信鲍鱼菇能强化体质。在降低血压和胆固醇上,也有非常显著的效果。

缺点:
含有少量嘌呤,不太适合于痛风病人。对于痛风病人,只要多吃水果和绿叶蔬菜,偶尔食用鲍鱼菇并无大碍。

芥末沾

木耳

黑木耳
也被称为"云耳"和"木耳"。黑木耳在中国食谱上已有多个世纪的历史。黑木耳本身没有太浓烈的味道,反而更善于吸收其他一起煮食的食品的味道,同时又维持其松脆的质感。

材料:
干黑木耳	80克
生抽	1 ½汤匙
糙米醋	5汤匙
芥末	1汤匙

方法:
1) 首先把黑木耳浸入热水直至软化(20分钟左右)。随后冲洗并沥干。
2) 把生抽、糙米醋和芥末一同搅拌成蘸酱。
3) 最后,把黑木耳和蘸酱置放在盘子上即可上桌。这是一道绝佳的开胃菜。

功效:
黑木耳性质平和,不燥亦不寒,对于抗凝血和降血压有非常显著的功效。木耳中的胶质可将残留在人体消化系统内的杂质吸附集中起来继而排出体外,而起清胃涤肠的作用。木耳中的多糖更是有抗癌、防癌的作用。

缺点:
无明显缺点。

拔丝

地瓜（番薯）

地瓜（番薯）
其貌不扬的番薯其实是拥有多种健康好处的神奇宝库。一直以来番薯被认定为穷人米饭的代替品，因为它有着与米饭大多相同的复合碳水化合物、纤维、胡萝卜素、维他命以及矿物质的营养来源。除此，番薯也有显著的抗氧及消炎的好处，更透过其甜味来帮助人们维持血糖。

材料：
番薯	500克	红糖	50克
植物油	5汤匙	热开水	½杯
芝麻	2汤匙		

方法：
1) 先将洗净的番薯去皮，再切成小块。再将切好的番薯块下油锅炸熟至呈金黄色。倒去大部分油，只留下一汤匙的油量。
2) 将糖在热水里溶解后，倒入锅内与炸好的番薯块和芝麻搅拌直至糖浆和芝麻完全包覆番薯块。随后即取出番薯块便可上桌。切记不要将糖浆煮得太久因为这将使整道菜变苦。
3) 上桌前，碟子上必须抹上一点油以免番薯块粘在碟面。贴士：番薯块很有可能会粘牙，因此你可以在食用前先将番薯块轻轻的浸入冰水里。

功效：
番薯性质属微凉，不会引起身体发热，堪称世界排名第一的抗癌食品。它不但能够润肠通便，还能够清热生津，更是减肥排毒的无上精选。

缺点：
容易引起腹胀或者产生胃酸。然而煮熟了的番薯就不会引起类似的问题。另一做法是可在食用番薯时喝开水或果汁。

凉拌

番薯叶

番薯叶
番薯叶也和番薯带来同样的益处（查阅第99页），更甚的是番薯叶减低了腹胀和胃酸增加的副作用。

材料：

番薯叶	200克	生抽	1汤匙
糙米醋	1汤匙	芥末	1茶匙
植物油	1汤匙	花椒	½汤匙
盐和黑椒粒	适量		

方法：
1) 首先将辣椒油弄好。把油倒进锅里待热，再把花椒放入油中爆香，直至花椒呈金黄色。接着把花椒从锅中取出后即可弃之。
2) 将番薯叶放入滚水里烫30秒后再放入冷水里（室内温度）。沥干后暂置一旁并加上适量的盐。
3) 随后把番薯叶置入一个碗中。加入辣椒油、生抽、糙米醋和芥末一起拌和后即可食用。

功效：
番薯叶与番薯有着相同的疗效，但是却没有番薯所拥有的副作用。番薯叶含有大量对身体有益的叶绿素，某些功能甚至优于番薯。对于抗癌、防癌、减肥、排毒尤其有显著的功效，更是糖尿病患者的首选食材。

缺点：
番薯叶唯一的缺点是一旦煮熟，其养分就被破坏。生的番薯叶打成汁是最具功效的，只是难以下咽。你可以把番薯叶和你喜爱的水果一同打成汁，这样就可减少难饮的口味。

凉拌

什锦

黄瓜

黄瓜原产于印度并在西亚地区种植超过3000年。黄瓜在公元前2世纪被带入中国，当时它被称为胡瓜。随后在五胡十六国时侯赵皇帝石勒君临天下之时，"胡"字被禁用，也因此胡瓜从此被称为黄瓜。黄瓜在传统中国医术的使用第一次的记载是在公元前7世纪。

材料：

黄瓜切成薄片	300克	糙米醋	2汤匙
豆皮	200克	植物油	4汤匙
金针菇	60克	花椒	1汤匙
粉丝	50克	辣椒粉	2汤匙
蒜头切碎	5瓣	香菜切碎	20克
盐和红糖	适量		

方法：

1）把金针菇的根部切除再放入滚水里烫30秒。随后沥干，暂置一旁。
2）把粉丝放入滚水里直至粉丝软化（5分钟）。随后沥干，暂置一旁。
3）要弄成辣椒油，就先把植物油倒入锅中待热。再把花椒放入锅中爆香直至花椒呈金黄色。接着把花椒从锅中取出后即可弃之。
4）把刚烫过滚水的金针菇和粉丝与其余的材料搅拌，并加入适量的盐和红糖。上桌前再倒入辣椒油即可。

功效：

黄瓜性质寒凉，能清热解毒、生津止渴。可用于治疗咽喉肿痛和发热、止渴，也常用于减肥。黄瓜内所含的营养成分，大多都可以用以抵抗肿瘤，而在抗癌蔬菜排行榜上，黄瓜排名第十三。

缺点：

脾胃寒凉的人要注意，吃后容易腹泻。

清炒

西兰花

西兰花
西兰花也是一种具抗氧化作用和植物化学物质的优质蔬菜。它相信于2000年前源自于意大利，当时被认为是野生卷心菜。

材料：
西兰花切成小花	300克
洋葱切成半后再切成薄片	1颗（中等大小）
姜切成薄片	2寸
生抽	1汤匙
植物油	2汤匙
盐和红糖	适量

方法：
1) 将洗净的西兰花后放入预先煮滚的开水氽烫一分钟，西兰花的颜色即变亮青色。将西兰花取出并放入一个装冷水的碗里，随后沥干它，并暂置一旁。
2) 在锅里放入少许的油，待锅热后把洋葱和姜加入爆香，直至闻到洋葱和姜的香气后再倒入生抽。
3) 最后，将沥干的西兰花放入锅里，并与姜和洋葱一起翻炒，再加入适量的盐和红糖。随后即可食用。

功效：
西兰花性质属微凉，在食疗上有补肾、壮骨、健脑和胃的功效。可以用于治疗因久病导致的身体虚弱、耳鸣和健忘。同时强健虚弱的脾胃，帮助清理隐藏在血管内的垃圾，除此之外，还能协助人体预防和抵抗癌症，在众多抗癌蔬菜里名列前茅，排名第三。

缺点：
西兰花营养价值虽高，但烹煮时间的长短拿捏非常重要，烹煮时间不宜过久，因为高温加热的过程中会导致西兰花失去部分的营养成分。

烧

茄子

茄子
茄子的生产地环绕印度、中国、缅甸、东南亚、寮国和越南地域,也因此茄子有不少的别名如源自法国的"aubergine"和葡萄牙的"brinjal"。茄子自古就被种植在亚洲。阿拉伯商人将茄子带到欧洲,接着西班牙人与葡萄牙人将它带到南美洲。

材料:
茄子去蒂	4个(中等大小)	蒜头切碎	3瓣
洋葱切碎	1颗	豆瓣酱	4茶匙
姜片切碎	3寸	植物油	3汤匙
盐和红糖	适量	过滤水	100毫升

方法:
1) 将茄子洗净并弄干。
2) 将茄子放入油锅煎至整条茄子平均地呈金黄色和香脆,火不宜太大以避免煎焦。
3) 然后放入洋葱、姜、蒜、豆瓣酱爆香。确保茄子的外皮完好不破裂。
4) 加入适量的水,盖锅小火煮十分钟,并加入适量的盐和红糖。接着将切碎的蒜头、洋葱和青瓜装饰后即可上桌。

功效:
生性属凉,具有清热止血、消肿止痛的功效。一般上用于改善各类的溃疡、便秘、高血压。茄子的皮拥有非常高的养分。抗癌蔬菜里,茄子排名第七。在马来西亚,我们称之为矮瓜。坊间盛传食用茄子对眼睛不好的说法。这是没有根据的,请勿轻信。

缺点:
容易让脾胃虚寒,哮喘病人千万不要食用。

苦 瓜

烧豆腐

苦瓜

苦瓜也被称为苦中之王。苦瓜在中国传统医术以及印度到亚马逊与撒哈拉都占有特别的位置。中国著名医师和药理学家李时珍（公元1518年-1593年）在其《本草纲目》中描述苦瓜为带苦味、无毒性、具去邪热、缓解疲劳以及降火明目功效的蔬菜。

材料：

苦瓜切成一寸长条状	2条		
嫩豆腐切成小块状	3块	洋葱切成薄片	½颗（中等大小）
豆瓣酱	3汤匙	植物油	2汤匙
姜片切成薄片	1寸	红糖	1汤匙
生抽	2汤匙	过滤水	200毫升
盐、糖	适量		

方法：

1）在锅内倒入植物油烧热，下洋葱姜爆香。
2）再倒入生抽、豆瓣酱、红糖翻炒。
3）放入苦瓜翻炒，加少许的水、盐；将已切成小块的豆腐放入，小火煮十分钟左右。
4）最后加入适量的盐和糖后，即可食用。

功效：

本性寒凉，具有清热解毒、降火明目的功效。适用于各种热性疾病、疖肿，更有显著的抗癌作用。苦瓜也是最佳的减肥食品之一，更是世界公认的脂肪杀手。

缺点：

脾胃寒凉者不宜食用，孕妇忌食。

酱醋炒

绿豆芽

绿豆芽

有哪一些蔬菜是既富有丰富营养，又可以自由在全球各地生长，不但无需泥土或肥料，而且生长至可食用的过程只需三到五天？答案当然是绿豆芽！中国的"药王"及"五谷之王"神农氏，远在公元前1282年，就已经在书中记载了这一些。

材料：

绿豆芽浸泡洗净	300克		
姜切成薄片	1寸左右		
洋葱切片	½个（中等大小）	植物油	1汤匙
海盐	½茶匙	生抽	1汤匙
红糖	½茶匙	糙米醋	4汤匙

方法：
1) 热油，爆香姜和葱，待颜色微黄时，加入生抽。
2) 将火调大，加入绿豆芽、盐和糖（用少许水调稀）。翻炒约30秒。
3) 最后加入醋，翻炒几秒钟。闻到香味后，熄火、起锅，即可食用。

功效：
豆芽本性微寒，能清热解毒、通脉利水、祛湿通便。传统医师常用它来改善目赤肿痛、口舌生疮，同时也可以降血脂，软化血管，缓解便秘，更有抗癌作用。

缺点：
因性质偏寒，不易于消化，脾胃虚寒的人不适合食用。

姜丝炒

芦笋

芦笋
芦笋的历史十分悠久。在阿比修斯（Apicius）于公元三世纪所著的古老食谱中，就已经提及了芦笋这种食材。甚至远在公元前三千年的古埃及建筑物的中楣上，也都绘有芦笋的图像。法王路易十七也曾经将芦笋种在宫殿的温室内。白芦笋与我们通常看到的绿芦笋其实来自同一种植物，不同的只是在种植白芦笋的时候，人们会将其根茎覆盖起来，以保留其白色。世界上最大的芦笋生产国为中国，但其出口量却排名世界第二，仅次于秘鲁。

材料：
芦笋	300克	姜切成薄片	1寸左右
生抽	1汤匙	盐	适量
植物油	3汤匙	红糖	少许

方法：
1) 洗净和沥干芦笋，再将之切段，长度约一寸半（4公分）左右。
2) 将水煮开，把芦笋置入锅内，烫约一分钟左右，捞起、沥干。煮芦笋不宜过久，以防它变成糊状。
3) 将油烧热，爆香姜，再下生抽。随即倒入芦笋，一起翻炒至均匀。
4) 起锅前加上少许盐和糖，即可食用。

功效：
芦笋生性寒凉，有清热生津、利水通淋的作用。经常食用对心脏病、高血压、心率过速、疲劳症、水肿、膀胱炎、排尿困难等病症有一定的疗效。此外，芦笋对心血管病、血管硬化、肾炎、胆结石、肝功能障碍和肥胖均有疗效。芦笋较许多蔬菜含有更丰富的维生素和微量元素。营养学家和素食界人士均认为它是健康食品和全面的抗癌食品。许多传统医师都会使用芦笋来治淋巴腺癌、膀胱癌、肺癌、肾结石、皮肤癌和白血症等。

缺点：
无明显缺点。

辣炒

卷心菜

卷心菜

卷心菜是具有四千年悠久历史的古老蔬菜，长久以来都广受希腊、罗马、中国及印度人的欢迎。早期的中国玉雕上都雕有卷心菜的图案，意味着它象征了财富和丰裕。在欧、亚两大洲，卷心菜也常被当成食物、药物和传统医疗材料。比如说，哺乳期的母亲会用卷心菜包裹乳房，以消除肿胀和疼痛。

材料：

卷心菜切成小片	500克	生抽	½汤匙
姜切成薄片	2寸左右	糙米醋	1汤匙
蒜头切碎	2瓣	红糖	½汤匙
干辣椒切半	6条	玉米淀粉	1½茶匙
花椒	1茶匙	水	200毫升
植物油	4汤匙	盐	适量

方法：

1）将生抽、糙米醋、糖、玉米淀粉、水和盐混合拌匀成调汁。
2）在炒锅内放入少量油，加入姜、蒜、辣椒和花椒爆香。
3）加入卷心菜翻炒，看到卷心菜明显萎蔫的时候，倒入调好的酱汁，翻炒均匀出锅装盘。
4）注意火候一定要猛，在卷心菜的养分还未被破坏之前，就应该出锅了。

功效：

根据中医学，卷心菜自古以来就被用于加速创面的愈合，治疗胃溃疡，解除便秘和排毒减肥。此外，它也适合于治疗动脉硬化、胆结石和消化道溃疡。

缺点：

脾胃虚寒、腹泻者少食。解决方法是加入本食谱所介绍的材料一起烹煮，以中和其副作用。

至于其他调味料如醋、酱油、洋葱、蒜头和姜的药性特点,我们将在附录中解说。

关于这本书食谱

本书中的每一道食谱都是根据特定的标准筛选出来。好比说,这里所选用的蔬菜都是一些富有药效且最具抗病功能的蔬菜,种类也不单调。每一道菜的准备和烹煮方式都简易方便,材料也能轻易地获得。食谱的重点在于排毒、滋养、修复和疗愈。正如早前所说,蔬菜是天然的药物,而这本书就是为了让大家懂得透过烹饪享用这些蔬菜所给予的好处。

编写此书对我们来说,是一个美好的经验。我们也衷心希望它能带给你一个美好的烹饪经验。

吃出美味,吃出健康!

家中去除食物火毒法：

要去除液状药物的火毒，只需打开瓶盖，放入冰箱冷冻格约三至四天即可；外用的药膏若没去除火毒，敷在身上会起红点；去火毒法如上。如果你能依据以上做法去除油炸或烧烤类食品的火毒，就不必完全戒食，偶尔食用并无大碍，也还能帮助身体驱寒。

加入素食行列

素食者必须根据完整的素食计划，食用各类青菜、菌类、海菜类及豆类，以确保在日常饮食中摄取均衡的营养。

规律适量的饮食习惯

健康的饮食关键不仅在于食材的本身，饮食时间的规律性与摄取量也很重要，即准时进食，而非感到饥饿才进食。有的人不吃早餐，有的人则在睡前才进食，这都严重影响我们的健康。饮食的份量也是关键之一，只要吃到七八分饱，千万别吃到十分饱。

调味料的药性

调味料一般属热性，特别是用做火锅汤底的调味料，或者用做腌肉酱的香料。许多人都不懂其中隐藏的热气。在中国各地都有火锅或腌肉的专卖店，有些人特别爱吃甚至到了每餐必备的程度。他们在两三年后就得了糖尿病。这是因为调料的热性伤及内脏，使内脏无法正常运作所导致。这种现象十分普遍，人们一般认为是肉吃多而引起，其实香料才是罪魁祸首。

比如说：八角、小茴香、草果、桂皮、丁香、白叩、胡椒、花椒、生姜、葱、蒜、辣椒都是偏热的。这些香料组合后弄成的腌肉酱美味无比，偶尔适量食用，可帮助我们驱除寒气；对于经常喝冷饮的人，这些调味料还能达到保胃的功效。

它们含有多种维生素、矿物质和各类植物化学成分，能补充、滋养及加强我们的内脏，同时也有助于对抗疾病。

这些食材对身体健康非常有利，但切记，请尽量避免单一性及油炸食物。

单一性的食物难以长久食用
每天食用同一道菜肴是非常无聊的。人们有时必须食用某种特定的蔬菜来治疗一些特定的病症。日子久了，他们很自然地就会对日复一日食用的食物感到厌倦。这个时候，往往就是患者转而求助于西药的时候了。所以，患者应尽可能选择更多样化的食物，而不是长期选择单一性的食物。

油炸食品导致火毒伤身
我们都了解油炸食品对身体不好，主要是因为食物经过高温处理后，会产生一种致癌的物质。古人虽然不懂这是什么东西，但总算也总结出"火毒"的理论。

我以前在制药的过程中也发现相同的现象。那些经长时间煎煮的药物，一旦让病人吃了以后就会出现上火（内热）的症状，但如果经过特别处理后就不会有大碍。

古人去火毒的方法有三种，
（一）磁坛封闭沉入井中两至三天。
（二）放在地面阴凉处或挖坑埋藏。
（三）外用的膏剂直接置在冷水中浸泡。

只要依据以上方式处理那些需要长时间高温处理的食物，就不会出现上火的现象。一般上，保健食品本身是不会引起内热现象的，然而由于许多医师在制药过程中没有遵守以上程序，才无法去除火毒。

前言
简单却令人惊喜的小书

这本书主要为大家介绍一些简单的素食烹饪方法。然而，这本看似简单的食谱，却一点儿也不简单。它其实是一本成功对抗现代文明病如癌症、糖尿病及肥胖症的策略小书。现代化的社会发展延伸出的其中一项副作用就是"富贵病"，如糖尿病和肥胖症的普遍化。不良的饮食习惯及食用过多加工食物不仅很难维持健康的体魄，还会导致肥胖症、糖尿病及其他相关问题日渐增多。此外，癌症更是不分贫富贵贱，给每一个人带来威胁。

人们在面对这些问题时，往往会选择西药和侵入性治疗作为首要的治疗方式。然而，传统中医所使用的方式，则着重于多管齐下；如做内在调理，首先要排出体内的毒素，然后再滋补内脏，好让它们拥有足够的力量来对抗疾病。

健康食物如水果和蔬菜都是天然的药物。它们都拥有独特的药性成分和功能。如今，使用天然食材来预防常见的疾病，已经成为一个促进健康的有效方法。

仁波切说过："人有时会忘了吃药，却不会忘了进食。这是人的天性。我们每天都必须进食，如果我们所吃的食物都拥有治病的作用，那肯定比任何药物都来得更好。"

把蔬菜当成药物？听起来可能有些牵强，许多人也对此持有怀疑的态度。然而，无数事实证明，食疗的效果是显而易见的，它甚至还可以媲美许多专用医疗药物。例如：木耳能散瘀血，有助于疏通阻塞的心脏血管，同时可帮助降低胆固醇，缓解便秘；芦笋则是众所周知的抗癌蔬菜，在中国，已经有人将芦笋的萃取物用来当治疗癌症的辅助品；卷心菜可以修复胃溃疡，对促进伤口愈合极为有效；菠菜有补血通便的功效，而芹菜则能协助降低血压。

除此之外，番薯的块茎和叶子都拥有丰富的营养成份，有助于对抗许多疾病。事实上，本书所使用的蔬菜如黄瓜、冬瓜、茄子等都是抗疾病食物中的战士。

作者简介
姜忠医师

姜忠姜医师，于1975年出生在中国。自幼便痴迷于古中医学，学习范围广泛，对于各家各派的医学范畴，皆有涉及和研究。姜医师正式在1998年毕业于中国吉林省长春中医学院，以此之后经历更是丰富；曾于吉林省洮南市十二药店坐堂三年，实习于中医的抓药、开方、配药等工作；也曾自开诊所两年，姜医师不为余力的临床实习了许多不同的病痛案例，让姜医师精湛的医术更上一层楼。

2001年起创办自然疗法保健院，主要从事气功治疗、针灸、推拿、刮痧、艾灸、外用药物等等天然疗法。更以'不服用药物'，而能促进健康、预防疾病为保健院的最大特点，再配合上饮食疗程，多年来姜医师证实了给各方人士，以此天然疗法确能治疗多种顽强疾病。同年，姜医师也在吉林省洮南市创办推拿学校。多年来，培育了不少推拿界的精英，造福广大的人群。

2005年来到东南亚，活跃于新加坡、马来西亚、泰国、越南等地区。间断性的，在东南亚已经行医超过四年多了。姜医师在东南亚一带，最主要诊治心脑血管疾病（中风后遗症）、糖尿病、颈肩综合症等，也着重于癌症病人的身心调养。

姜医师特别提倡西医诊断，可是却擅长用较无化学性质反效果的中医药作为治疗手段，尤其重视"瘀不去则新不生的理念"。所谓的"瘀"包括了瘀血、瘀痰、郁热、瘀气，而对城市人来说最为普遍的便秘，其实也是一种瘀的现象。去除了这些瘀滞，才能真正的产生新能量。这也是本书以排毒清热为主的原因之一。

121

尊贵的詹杜固仁波切
克切拉佛教团体精神导师

序
尊贵的詹杜固仁波切

在现代生活中，加工食物让我们的生活变得更方便：我们轻易地就能买到包装及处理好的食物，而我们需要做的只是再加热便可食用。结果，我们在这样的饮食中牺牲了自己的健康。我为此感到内疚，因为我也因这样的饮食习惯而赔上了自己的健康。我肯定除了我之外，仍然有不少人同样经历过如此的情况。

我遇见一个煮得一手好菜、精于针灸和医治我身体状况的医师。遵从他的劝告和治疗，我的健康状况改善许多。有一天在和这位医师聊天时偶然发现他会下厨。他解释说儿时居住的村庄里因没有太多的肉，故此人们都是素食者。村庄里的人们利用手上仅有的蔬菜做各种搭配，而成果都挺美味的。

享誉中外的中国传统医术讲究的是体内阴（寒）和阳（热）的协调。这本食谱专设的重点在于个人体内的阴阳协调。我个人发现食谱中的每道菜都非常美味、清淡，虽有饱足感，却不会有饱涨的感觉。

我觉得有必要将这些古代珍贵的治疗法和特别的食谱广泛地在世界各地流传。我认为这本食谱会满足到那些嘴刁但也希望自己能吃得健康的人。食谱中每道菜的制作过程都非常简易和经济，非常适合喜欢方便和低开销的人参阅，因为食谱中没有一道菜是属昂贵的。

我希望人人都能拥有健康的身躯，没有疾病苦痛并保持长寿。我更希望每位读者能从我一位医术高明的中医师兼好友姜医师所编写的食谱中获益。在此至上万分谢意。

詹仁波切

目录

尊贵的詹杜固仁波亲序	122 - 123
作者简介	120 - 121
前言	116 - 119
食谱 1：辣炒卷心菜	114 - 115
食谱 2：姜丝炒芦笋	112 - 113
食谱 3：酱醋炒绿豆芽	110 - 111
食谱 4：苦瓜烧豆腐	108 - 109
食谱 5：烧茄子	106 - 107
食谱 6：清炒西兰花	104 - 105
食谱 7：凉拌什锦	102 - 103
食谱 8：凉拌番薯叶	100 - 101
食谱 9：拔丝地瓜	98 - 99
食谱 10：芥末沾木耳	96 - 97
食谱 11：鲍鱼菇	94 - 95
食谱 12：凉拌菠菜	92 - 93
食谱 13：海带炖豆腐	90 - 91
食谱 14：竹笋炒西兰花	88 - 89
食谱 15：安神银耳羹	86 - 87
食谱 16：忘忧汤	84 - 85
食谱 17：排毒粥	82 - 83
食谱 18：利水冬瓜粥	80 - 81
素食中的佛法	78 - 79
食谱 19：蕃茄炒蛋	76 - 77
食谱 20：炸南瓜	74 - 75
食谱 21：水饺	72 - 73
鸣谢	71
克切拉团体介绍	70
克切拉媒体出版社简介	69
克切拉世界和平中心——亚洲的灵修圣地	68
词汇表——活出健康基本知识	65 - 67
词汇表海报	附件
英文翻译	01 - 64

Copyright © 2011 Kechara Media & Publications
版权所有。除供学术文章及书评作简短摘录外，未经克切拉媒体出版社书面允许，任何人皆不可以任何形式擅自复制或盗用本书内容。

出版社的话：此书内容仅供做一般参考用途，不能作为或取代其他专业意见、医疗建议，或诊断及治疗手段。

克切拉媒体出版社有限公司
41-2A & 41-2B, 1st Floor
Jalan PJU 1/3C
SunwayMas Commercial Centre
47301 Petaling Jaya
Selangor, Malaysia

电话：(+603) 7805 5691
传真：(+603) 7805 5690
电邮：kmp@kechara.com
网站：www.kechara.com/kmp

国际标准书号：978 967 5305 48 5

艺术总监：Andrew James Boon
摄影：Lee Kheng San (Kechara InMotion)
翻译：Low Kar Wai
编辑：Saras Manickam
设计排版：Wong Yek Hao

印刷：Times Offset (M) Sdn Bhd, Malaysia

天天健康好膳食

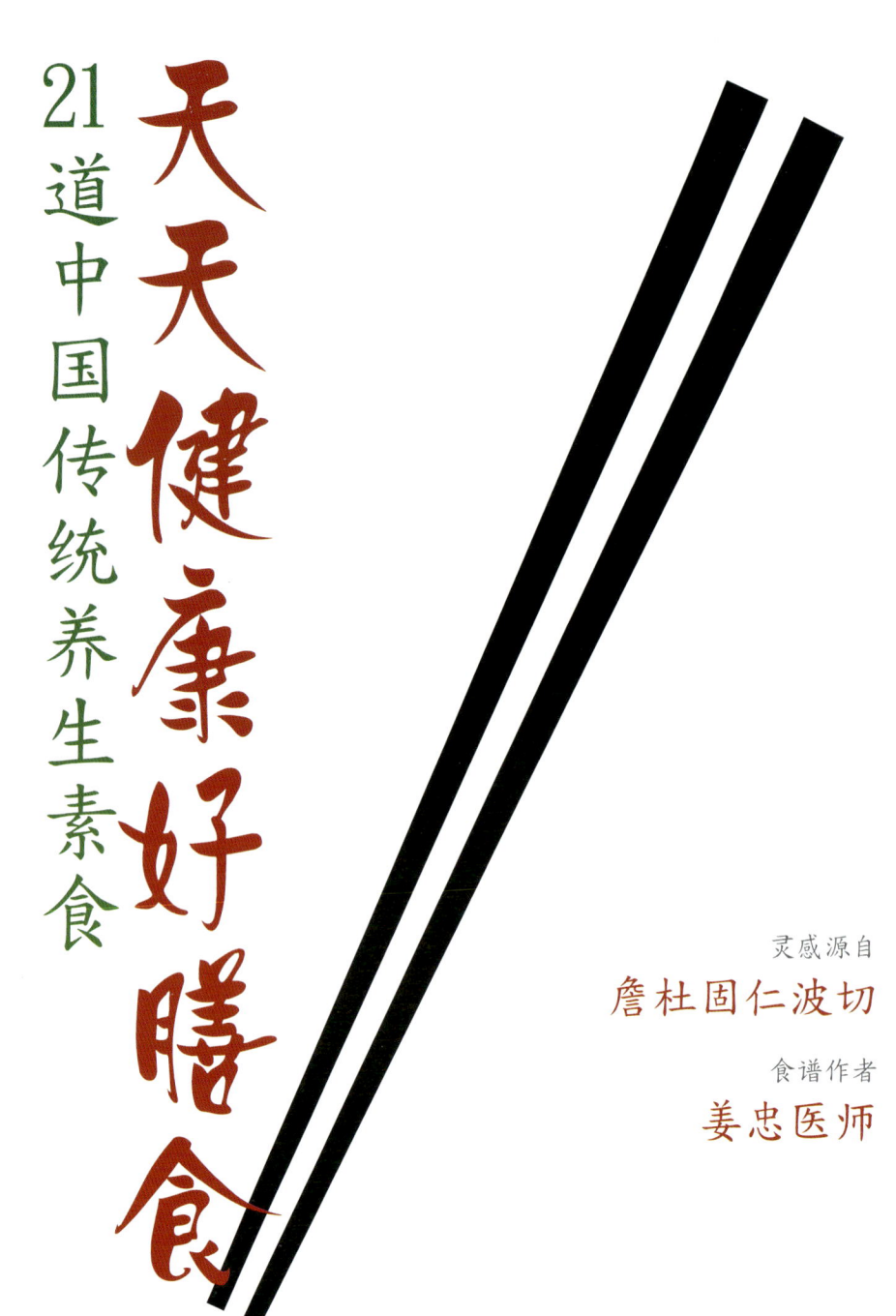

21道中国传统养生素食

灵感源自
詹杜固仁波切

食谱作者
姜忠医师

克切拉媒体出版社
2011

克切拉媒体出版社出版的其他詹杜固仁波切著作
（按出版日期排列）

摘下修身之果～108精言良诫，
詹杜固仁波切著，2010年

宗喀巴大师套装书，
詹杜固仁波切 著，2010年

宁静（第二版），
詹杜固仁波切著，2010年

一切更棒，
詹杜固仁波切著，2009年

一切如初，
詹杜固仁波切著，2009年

一切业造，
詹杜固仁波切著，2009年

宁静（第一版），
詹杜固仁波切著，2009年

念念当下，
詹杜固仁波切著，2009年

克切拉媒体出版社出版的其他书籍

金刚瑜伽母及尼泊尔其他圣地，叶师杰构思，
黎国圆撰写，2010年

金甲衣护法套装书，
郭月谊著，2010年

宗喀巴大师传（漫画版），
郭月谊著，林钷晴绘，2009年

欲知详情，或有意购买以上书籍，请浏览 www.kechara.com/kmp
克切拉媒体出版社同时也出版英文书籍。